THE REBUILT MIND

All the best!

THE REBUILT MIND
ACCEPT. DEVELOP. ACHIEVE.

SHAUN FITZGERALD

Shaun.

All the best!

First published in Great Britain in 2022

Hardback ISBN: 978-1-7390985-1-3
Trade Paperback ISBN: 978-1-7390985-3-7
eBook ISBN: 978-1-7390985-2-0

CONTENTS

THE REBUILT MIND

PREFACE

*"When you experience a negative mindset, you need to push
beyond your limits to find your inner positivity."*

- Shaun Fitzgerald

Welcome to my book. My name is Shaun Fitzgerald and I am a profoundly Deaf. I embrace my Deafness and even when going through adversity, at the back of my mind buried deep, was the realisation that I am proud to be Deaf.

When exploring the idea of writing this book, I canvassed a few people that I knew for their opinion and whether I should write this book or not. To put it bluntly the feedback I received was as follows:

"You are not intelligent enough to write a book"

"Nobody will be interested as your life experiences are not that important"

"Who wants to read a book about a Deaf person and their issues with the education system and life in general"

All positive and glowing sorts of encouragement?

This was why I decided to go ahead and ignore the comments that had been made and to prove that I could and would write a book about my life to date.

The first issue was, I am a native British Sign Language (BSL) user. English is not my first language. An easy way to explain this is to imagine that you are French and asked to write a book in German. Immediately you have an issue, in that, as a BSL user, I did and do not have the skills to write in English. I needed someone to interpret my words into English and then to write the book for me. The words in this book and its contents were all signed to my interpreter, who in turn then transcribed them into written English.

As you can imagine, it took a long time to achieve what has been written. Many hours were spent going over the details and content and clarification of meaning and intent, including the emotional aspects of my story.

I have written this book based on my own experiences of the education system and life in general as a Deaf person. I suspect others have had similar experiences, but my story looks at life from a Deaf perspective. The book looks at the impossible attempts to access a normal education, my progress or lack of, through my formative years as a child and teenager.

My life was in turmoil and every time my mother and I tried to access help from the professionals, we were faced with barriers constantly.

The barriers that I faced, resulted in me considering and nearly taking my own life. I was at my wits end. I had no direction in life. I had decided to end my life as I thought that would solve all my problems and with me not being around, would make things a lot easier.

I have written this book as an insight into the problems and issues that Deaf people can and have faced. It is a guide to what went wrong and, what is wrong with the system we had in place and sadly, still have today.

I am not saying it is all bad but there is room for improvement. The solution is not included in my book. The answers are out there and I guess they are for others to reflect on and see how things can be improved.

Any improvement would have a positive effect on someone's mental health. For example, equal access to education can improve a child's wellbeing and mental health, but there are still so many barriers to equal access to education for Deaf children. Support for Deaf children has come a long way since I was in school, however there still needs to be so much more focus on this. Ensuring that Deaf children have access to education in their own language (BSL) is so important, not just for language and academic development, but to also enable them to learn about their own culture and community from a young age - there are a lot of differences between hearing and Deaf culture's.

I hope you find this book informative and if I asked myself what one thing the reader should take away from this book, it would be, that they get a small insight into what being Deaf is like within our education system and life in general.

CHAPTER ONE

EARLY YEARS

"My mission in life is not merely to survive, but to thrive."

- Maya Angelou

I was diagnosed as Deaf when I was 2 years old. Throughout my childhood, and into adulthood, I faced barriers every single day of my life. Barriers that other people may or may have not faced. Sadly, I had very little interaction with other Deaf children or adults until my later school years, due to my family unfortunately not being given the right support or guidance on where to connect with the Deaf community. Interaction with hearing children and adults was also limited, due to the frustration of not being able to communicate effectively with them.

I believe every child has a right to access quality education, and whilst researching material for this book I came across a quote that reflects this statement very well. Nelson Mandela said…

"Education is the most powerful weapon which you can use to change the world."

I wanted to have the same opportunity as others but unfortunately, that wasn't going to happen until I was much older.

This book is about how I managed to change from a life of adversity, into one that is now of progress and fulfilment.

Adversity is described as:

'A state of hardship, difficulty, or misfortune that one deals with in life. There are several types of adversity that one can face and facing adversities in life can break or make a person.'

Has my life been one of hardship? Looking back, I guess it was. I suffered through lack of a decent education. Communication felt impossible because I was surrounded by people who were hearing and speaking English. I could not hear what was being said. My peers would interact all the time and I was the one sitting on my own. I felt isolated and was missing the opportunity to interact. It left me feeling miserable as I did not feel a part of anything.

Looking back, I feel my initial experience of the education that was available to me was inadequate, this in turn affected my ability to communicate effectively as I wasn't taught BSL until later on in my childhood and I wasn't able to lipread well as a child. It was exhausting, I sat at the front of a class, trying to work out what words were being spoken by the teacher and my peers. I did not have the lip-reading skills to be able to learn sufficiently.

Sadly, it wasn't just myself that wasn't given the chance to learn BSL from a young age, due to inadequate education and access, my family were also affected. I was the only one in my family that was Deaf, and all my family were hearing. Due to the lack of support and education, the only way we could communicate with each other was through hand gestures and pointing.

There were times that I felt I wished I would have been born different, but I now embrace my deafness and I am proud to be Deaf. Regardless of being Deaf or hearing, we each face our own ups and downs in life.

The issues I've faced have been to do with lack of understanding. The needs of a Deaf child during their formative years require professional knowledge. I was put into a school with no communication support and no assistance from the teachers to try and help me get better access to the curriculum.

It all started when I was very young. My mother witnessed many aggressive outbursts at the age of 2. I would get frustrated and throw things around the house. My mother told me that on one occasion, I upended a large table, and she was astonished about the strength and anger I was showing. She decided that it might be best to take me to the local GP. The GP according to my mother's recollection, examined me and was not sure what was going on at the time.

Being a 2-year-old Deaf boy was difficult as there were conversations being had and I had no access or understanding about what was being said. This made me even more frustrated, and I expressed this through violent outbursts.

My mother was a single parent, I never knew my father and to this day have never concerned myself with looking for him or finding out more about him either. She wanted to understand what was going on with me and my behaviour, but with limited access to the right support she didn't know where to turn, so started with the GP.

The GP noticed that when he was talking to me, that I was not responding and just looking around the room. He clapped his hands loudly behind me and I showed no reaction. After speaking with my mother, they agreed that something was not quite right. The GP decided to refer me to the local Audiology clinic at our local hospital.

Arriving for the appointment an Audiologist took me into a room and sat me down and explained to me what was going to happen. At that time, I had no idea I was Deaf and all I could see was this man moving his lips and waving his arms around. He eventually gave up and spoke with my mum. There was a lot of head nodding and shaking of heads. I had no idea what was going on.

The man came over to me and gave me two plungers that I held in each hand. Later I discovered this was because the left-hand plunger was for the left ear and the right-hand one for the right ear. The man went behind a screen with my mother, and I sat there looking around and wondering what was next. After a short time, the man came back around and took each plunger and pressed them several times and then gave them back to me and walked off. After a while the plungers were taken off me. It later transpired they had determined I was profoundly Deaf. I had no idea what this meant.

There are 4 levels of Hearing loss or Deafness that are used to describe a person's hearing capability or lack of. They are Mild, Moderate, Severe, and Profound. These descriptions are sorted into dB which refers to the word decibel. To get an understanding of what each level of Deafness is, it might be worth giving an example for each one:

Mild hearing loss (21-40 dB) this would for example be, not hearing a clock ticking or unable to hear a dripping tap. This kind of hearing loss can be normally rectified using hearing aids. In younger children this can be effective as it helps to clarify certain parts of speech.

Moderate hearing loss (41-55 dB) this would for example be, not understanding normal speech, unable to hear a doorbell, or unable to hear a telephone ring. This can be helped using hearing aids.

Severe hearing loss (56-90 dB) this would for example be, if a person was not using hearing aids, it would be quite impossible to hear and or understand normal speech.

Profound hearing loss (90+ dB) this would mean for example, people would be unable to hear 'soft' sounds from 90-120 dB. This would mean they would not benefit completely from using hearing aids. A person may not even be able to hear loud sounds like an airplane engine, or fire alarms. High frequency loss affects the consonant sounds in speech whereas low frequency loss affects the vowels, loss in both means you're going to be unable to hear speech effectively.

People with this degree of hearing loss would not be able to hear speech and would rely on lip reading, gestures, or other visual clues. Some people will choose to use Sign Language as their main method of communication.

My hearing loss is at the end of the Profound hearing loss scale, my loss is more than 120 dB. Therefore, in my early years without access to speech or communication, life was very frustrating for me, and it helped to explain my outbursts of excessive anger.

It was discovered that hearing aids could be used to support my hearing slightly, this was only a very small amount and I found that I could only use my hearing aids effectively in a small group or 1:1 setting where I had full eye contact and I could see the person talking. If I was in a noisy place or too many people, the hearing aids were of no use, due to too much background noise and that would cause me more stress. Without the advantage of hearing words my brain has no prior knowledge of how words or speech, sound. This results in my voice and sounds being very guttural. Unlike some Deaf people who have had the benefit of hearing speech sounds and akin to muscle memory, their brain has managed to store these sounds so when later in life, their hearing deteriorates, they can still repeat speech sounds that can be possibly understood.

My brain hasn't had the experience of processing sounds and speech patterns. My speech and words are not clear and the pronunciation of words when you have no experience of the sound, makes speaking clearly impossible for me.

During my younger years when I didn't know BSL nor had the ability to hear properly, one of the things I struggled most with, was that this made me feel that there were huge barriers between myself and social inclusion within my peer group and community. This quote below really resonates with me, not that I think that everyone thinks this way, but this is how I felt when I was younger and unfortunately some members of society still feel that same - this is why more awareness is needed.

Marion Ross said:

"The thing about hearing loss is that no one can see it. Most people are so impatient; they just assume that the person with hearing loss is being rude, or slow-witted"

CHAPTER TWO

INTRODUCTION TO EDUCATION

"Education is the key to opportunity in society, and the equality of educational opportunity must be the birth right of every citizen."

- Lyndon B Johnson

My mother tried to cope with my deafness until I was 5, I was then sent to a mainstream school. At school, there were no discussions about extra provision, or assessments done to ascertain what it was I could and could not hear or comprehend.

The school experience was awful as I sat in a room full of my peers and watched this person stood at the front moving their lips and children laughing and joining in while I sat there on my own. I tried to copy the children around me so when they laughed, I laughed. Unfortunately, with the delayed response of laughing when others had stopped, I appeared to others as being 'weird'.

At break and lunchtimes, it was even worse because when I tried to join in with the others, they would turn their backs and walk away as they didn't want to play with me.

I remember during my early years; I missed a lot of information and was not privy to conversations in general. Nothing was conveyed to me, and I was pretty much left in the dark. It appeared that the effort to communicate with me, in the eyes of the teachers, was just 'not worth it'. It was too much of an effort to even try to 'get through' to me.

Looking back, it saddens me to think, this was how things were. I would like to think that nowadays, things have improved vastly. Schools now have access to more information and generally, a diagnosis of deafness etc is identified early. Once this has been identified, measures are usually put in place to ensure that the child has an equal opportunity to learn and to be educated alongside their hearing peers. Communication support is decided and put in place to ensure that communication is available from the start.

Schools will normally provide a person who will work alongside the child and within a primary school setting, will be with that child from reception through to year 6 and leaving school at the age of 11.

Within this time, the child will have access to the same information their hearing peers have, unlike my situation, due to the lack of intervention and communication support.

I remember being at school with a young girl, who I will call Amanda *(This is not her real name, but the author was unable to seek permission for her real name to be used in this book, and therefore, would not want to cause upset with those who knew her)* She was in the same class as me and was poorly. I later discovered that she had been born with a medical condition. She was in my class for a while, and I really liked her. One day she did not come to school, and no one told me why she was not there. I did not see her for the rest of the time I was at that school.

There was no information passed onto me and I was absolutely in the dark as to why she wasn't at my school again. It wasn't until I was 16 that my mother told me she had died. I was shocked and very upset, as

I had not been told. I was extremely angry and demanded to know why my mum hadn't told me. She told me that when she died at 6 years old, she felt that telling me would be too traumatic for me to understand or handle.

I was furious because I discovered that my hearing peers all knew but no one had thought that I should be told. My mother showed me an Order of Service from her funeral, and it saddened me to find out she had died and that I had missed the opportunity to be informed of that fact.

This was the kind of life I suffered throughout. I was never informed of things that I ought to have been made aware of. People decided what I should and should not know. Nobody asked me my view on the matter, it was decided that 'adults' knew best. I am aware that this also happens with most children, deaf or hearing, but I felt as though I was at a disadvantage. Hearing children would possibly hear things later through peer-to-peer conversation. I would not have that benefit as my communication was limited, not only as I was Deaf, but due to lack of knowledge of

BSL, this made me feel even more so isolated from my family and friends.

Looking back, I do not believe that it was correct, not giving me access to important information like my friend dying was frustrating. I guess my mother like other parents, was trying to be protective. All parents have a big responsibility raising children, and I truly feel that my mother did her best, especially raising me as a single parent and facing the barriers we both faced with the lack of professional support.

Dr. Anita Gadhia-Smith, a Washington, D.C. psychiatrist who counsels individuals, couples, and families, offers her thoughts on the topic. She believes that no one size fits all.

The issue is complex. As Dr. Gadhia-Smith sees it, there is no one-size-fits-all manual for raising kids. *"First time parents will go through a trial an error process, and each child within a family may be very different,"* she says. *"In general, children do have very different levels of comprehension, depending on individual personality development and age."* (Dr. Anita Gadhia-Smith)

If this is the case, then my mother may have been correct at the time, when making her decision to withhold information about 'Amanda' dying. Dr. Gadhia-Smith said that children have different levels of comprehension.

It could be argued that due to my very limited communication ability, this impacted my level of understanding, and I was not ready nor able to comprehend what dying and death meant.

As for whether there's an age-appropriate version of the truth, Dr. Gadhia-Smith says that children under five cannot comprehend the complexity of life and relational issues that an older child can. *"The older the child, the greater the need for fully honest disclosure and guidance that will help the child integrate and set their own value system."*

Now that I am older, I realise that my mother did the right thing by waiting until I was aged 16 to tell me the truth, at aged 5 I would have been far too young and lacked the ability to understand clearly.

She did as best as she could as a single parent and I am grateful for that. My anger and annoyance are with the system. Somebody could have offered my mother some advice on how to deliver information to me. She received no support at all.

The time between 'Amanda' passing away and being told was nearly 10 years. Between her death and being told, my mother or others could have explained to me that she had passed away and spent some time explaining what death and dying meant. A big question is whether it is okay for parents to withhold information from their kids. Here is where it comes down to good judgement.

According to Dr. Gadhia-Smith "In general, it is not advisable to lie," However, it is not always advisable to tell all either.

I now understand that parents use their own inner guidance about what feels right to them as each child is different and this needs to be taken into account in all situations.

While I do agree with the fact that parents need to use their inner guidance in regards to what feels right in a situation, I do believe that sometimes it can be possible to impart sufficient evidence to explain a situation.

My mother along with people from both school and external agencies could have compiled an explanation, that both, helped me to understand and comprehend, whilst not causing undue worry and concern. The school and others were able to provide appropriate information to my hearing peers. I know this is correct as I have spoken with some of these children who were in my class and who had been told about the passing of 'Amanda'.

All in all, looking back, I feel that I was misinformed in a lot of situations, due to the lack of communication between myself, friends, family and professionals. I felt that this was unfair and left me, and even my family, not knowing.

This went on until I was aged around 10. I had 5 years of misery, bullying both physically and mentally, and a sense of total isolation. Even after school, once I was at home, there was nobody to communicate with. My mum tried her best, but she had no knowledge or experience with a Deaf child.

I remember when I was at primary school making a Mother's Day card for my mum. My mum used to take me to after school club to play pool and football. This was to try and help me build some confidence around others. I used to play for a local football team and my teammates used to communicate with me through gesture, mime, and a lot of hand waving.

During my childhood I coped by keeping myself occupied. I enjoyed sitting down with paper and pencils and draw cartoon characters. Some of these were of Dennis the Menace and Gnasher copied from my comics, some of both David Beckham and Cristiano Ronaldo. These were copied from photos I had. The drawing helped me to reduce any anger issues I had, and I also found the drawing relaxing.

When I was 11 years old, I moved to secondary school and joined a local football club who played their matches at the weekend. I enjoyed playing for the team and started to become a little more confidant around others. gesturing on the football pitch was a lot easier than trying to lip-read each other and it seemed to be successful.

Around the same time, I was into making things out of cardboard and remember making things like a mobile phone amongst other things. It helped me to focus my mind and I found it a good way of easing any stress or frustration I was going through at the time. One of the biggest problems was trying to communicate when in a group and at family gatherings etc. I struggled to understand what others were talking about and used to nod my head and smile most of the time. It was a way of coping at the time.

Knoors and Marschark (2014) noted that deaf students frequently are at risk regarding social and emotional learning *"due to more limited social-emotional experiences, social skills, and emotional maturity, any or all of which potentially can lead to negative impact on academic achievement."* This situation likely derives in large, from communication challenges inside and outside of the home that can affect the incidental acquisition of manners and other behaviours indicative of social maturity.

Parents and teachers also sometimes hold deaf children and other children with disabilities to less stringent rules and responsibilities compared with their hearing, typically developing age-mates *(Doren, Gau, & Lindstrom, 2012)*, another factor that could affect social maturity.

"Social maturity" broadly refers to age-appropriate social behaviour that reflects some degree of social competence. It represents the responsible

implementation of competent behaviour in interactions with others, resulting in appropriate and adaptive social functioning. Thus, social maturity includes components of social skills and social competence, along with the implementation of those skills in adaptive social interactions.

Social skills and social competence alone may not indicate maturity, because the former reflect ability/knowledge but not necessarily responsible activation of that ability/knowledge in behaviour. Similarly, social confidence may differ if the confidence *(which is based on internal appraisal of competence)* is not representative of actual skill or behaviour. In contrast, it requires not only skills and competence but also responsibility and activation (behaviour).

Some aspects of social maturity are taught explicitly in the home and in school in terms of familial and cultural values. To a much larger extent, social values and the behaviours associated with them are acquired incidentally through interactions and particularly interactions involving language *(Vygotsky, 1978, p. 27)*, with friends, classmates, teachers and strangers as well as family members.

As such, the issue of incidental learning as it is related to language, psychosocial functioning and knowledge of the world is of considerable importance to parents, teachers and researchers working with deaf children and youth.

A frequent explanation for deaf children's delays in language development, social development and academic achievement, is that their hearing losses prevent them acquiring knowledge relevant to those domains by overhearing the conversations of others as well as communication aimed at them.

Although it is difficult to quantify the effects of overhearing the language of others *(or not)*. The potential for improved hearing and spoken language interactions with diverse others may provide benefits to the development of social maturity.

If I look back I can see that, I didn't even know the basics for example, good morning, good afternoon etc. I had no understanding of the social norms of turn taking, the concept of please and thank you. In my later years I reflected on this and searched for some understanding of my behaviour.

Due to the lack of human connection, most feral children suffer mental impairments, diminished language ability, a lack of social skills and physical problems. During our formative years, we learn how to behave in accordance with our culture through a process called enculturation.

Enculturation is described by the Merriam Webster Dictionary as:

"The process by which an individual learns the traditional content of a culture and assimilates its practices and values."

As a Deaf child 30 years ago, I did not have access to the culture and norms of society. The language barrier was the main issue and without any clear communication method taught to me, I was socially isolated.

Through no fault of my own or my mother, I felt and still feel that we (my mother and I) were seriously let down.

There wasn't anyone from the education authorities or the school kicking down our door to help. In fact, the opposite was true, there were, from my mother's recollection of events, no extra effort to assist in ensuring I received a satisfactory education. It wasn't until I was 10 years old that intervention occurred.

I was at school one day when a person, who I later discovered was a Specialist Educational Needs Co-ordinator (SENCo) visited the school to speak with the teachers. It transpired; he was there to assess my needs. Finally, someone had recognised that I was not achieving what was expected at my age level. After the assessment, my mum was informed that I would be moving to another school where children with 'similar issues' as it was described, attended. The journey was an hour each morning and afternoon, adding 2 hours to my school day. I was only 10 and it resulted in me being very tired.

The first day I arrived and walked into the playground I could see children of various ages, 'waving' their hands and arms about. I was terrified and wondered what I was doing there. I thought it was a punishment for not doing well at my previous school. After a while it dawned on me that these children were also Deaf or Hard of Hearing (HoH) and were using gesture and British Sign Language (BSL). Everything was so visual, and I was able to understand the odd word here and there. It was a thing of beauty and made me feel very emotional.

During my time at my new school, I started to develop my understanding of sign language on a basic level. The first thing my new peers taught me was 'good morning, good afternoon, how are you, etc'. Along with these basic signs I also learnt swear words as a lot of kids of my age did.

My teacher was able to sign, and we had what was called a Communication Support Worker (CSW). This person was there to aid communication but at the same time, they were there to help me with my English and comprehension of what was being said. It was a revelation and what I would describe as a *'re-birth'*. I had finally found language and the ability, with help, to access it, albeit, at a basic level.

A basic level for me was like having the keys to the sweet shop. I didn't care that I was not functioning at a higher level. That was unimportant to me, because for the first time in 10 years, I could *'speak'*. I could be heard and seen.

After the first 10 years of my life, without overstating things, I was a person. Someone who existed, somebody who was recognisable and seen as on a level with my other peers. I used to rush home after school and bombard my mother with what I had learnt, seen, or 'heard' through a language which was visual. I didn't need to know how things sounded. All I knew was that objects and everyday things were real and had words and descriptions attached to them. There was no need to point and make noises at objects to make myself seen and heard. Now I had the start of a rich, colourful, expressive language. I wanted to learn everything in the first week which later, I realised was physically impossible, but at 10 years old it was an expectancy.

Along with language acquisition was knowledge. I had an insatiable appetite to learn as much as I could, in as little time as possible. My teachers showed concern as I was constantly on my feet, moving around the classroom, interrupting discussions, and totally lacking the social skills of turn taking. To me that was not important as I felt that I was *'owed'* 10 years of communication, 5 years plus of education, and a lifetime of being noticed and recognised.

The stay at this school only lasted a year as when I turned 11, it was time to move onto secondary education. The school was based in Hull. My newly acquired friends from my old school joined me in Hull and therefore I had people around me who I already knew. We were in a mainstream establishment of nearly 1,700 children of which, 99% were hearing. We were based in a Partial Hearing Unit (PHU).

The purpose of a PHU was for the Deaf children to meet up there first thing in the morning, check what was needed re support for the day, and to allow access to the CSW's and Teacher of the Deaf (TOD), for extracurricular support. If someone was struggling to keep up with their lessons etc, then they would be offered extra support at lunchtimes and after school. This had its disadvantages; if you needed support then you would have to forfeit the social interaction with your peers.

The PHU had a worse effect if you were attending because, some of the children *(hearing)* would see that you were requiring extra help and the fact, that you were Deaf, which led to situations where bullying occurred. Bullying not only occurred at school but was also evident in my social life. I remember around the age of 10/11 years old I joined my local scout group. I thought it would help me with life skills etc. I remember we went away on a camp with my scout troop, and I was really looking forward to it whilst at the same time, a little nervous as communication was going to be an issue.

My scout leaders could not sign and tried their best to commute with me through gestures. We arrived at camp and set up all the tents we were going to sleep in. I was with a group of boys I knew quite well and had seen them a lot at the scout meetings. We were out one day in rowing boats on the river, and I was quite nervous as I was not a good swimmer. As I was looking over the side, one of the boys pushed me and I fell in. I was panicking and thought I was going to drown but luckily, my scout leader grabbed hold of me and pulled me back into the boat. I was not sure which boy pushed me in but if I had not been pulled out, I would have possibly drowned.

After the boat incident we went back to our camp and had food. Our next adventure was to build a tent out of logs and bits of wood and bush and leaves. We gathered all the materials and joined it all together with string and rope. This we were told, was a skill that was useful if we were caught out in the wilderness.

Later that day we had to make a fire using 2 twigs and some material. The scout leader was trying to explain to me how to get the fire started, which was difficult as he couldn't sign and I couldn't hear him which resulted in not understanding what he was saying. Eventually, I gave up on trying to read his lips and opted to watch the boy next to me. After watching a few times, I understood how to rub the sticks together. After a while I managed to start the fire, and this made me very proud and increased my confidence and belief in myself. Watching others became a tried and tested way of learning and one I was to adopt for the rest of my secondary years. The trick was to make sure you watched the right students.

One evening we were messing about in our tent and the leader told us off. We waited until it was dark then climbed the tree above where the tent roof was supported by a rope, tied to a branch on the tree. We thought as a joke, we would untie the rope and see what happened. After the tent roof collapsed, we dived back inside our tent and waited for the yelling and telling off to happen. After a few minutes no one had come so, we peeped outside, and I crawled forward and looked inside the leader's tent.

They were both fast asleep and did not know the roof had collapsed. I thought at one stage that they were not breathing and panicked. But we realised after a while that they were both okay and we went back to our tent and after a while we all went to sleep. The next morning, we all got up and it was funny as the scout leaders had no idea how their roof had collapsed.

My next social venture was joining the local army cadets. As a Deaf person, they were worried due to health and safety and duty of care. I was given access to a rifle that could fire live rounds. I was put on a trial period and was monitored carefully.

I think I was there for around 6 months or more, and during one exercise I was told to stop and stay still and given other instructions which unfortunately, I never heard as the instructors were behind me. They decided this was too dangerous and apologised to me but told me I could not continue as a cadet. I fully understand their decisions now, but when I was a young lad who was so desperate to fit in and be accepted, the decision for me seemed harsh and discriminatory.

Socially, I was becoming more and more awkward. Which resulted in me feeling socially isolated. I was experiencing bullying both socially and educationally. Times were looking tough, and I could not see anything that looked to be positive, short, or long term. From my perspective I was thinking and believing, that life was absolutely fucking shit.

CHAPTER THREE

LIFE WAS A LIVING HELL

"Getting knocked down in life is a given. Getting up and moving forward is a choice."

- Zig Ziglar

While I was at the school, I received intolerable levels of bullying both emotionally and physically. The physical side of it was manageable to a level. The hardest, and the most lasting effect on me personally and I suspect, would be for others, was the emotional abuse.

Emotional abuse comes in many guises, it can best be described as:

"Any act, including confinement, isolation, verbal assault, humiliation, intimidation, infantilisation, or another treatment

that may diminish the sense of identity, dignity, and self-worth".
(The Awareness Centre LTD.)

In other words, emotional abuse is when the behaviour or comments of the other makes, you feel bad about yourself, when at heart you know you've got nothing to feel bad about.

There are several factors that are evident when and why bullying occurs. One of these is Peer Factor. The features of this are:

- to attain or maintain social power or to elevate the bully's status in their peer group.

- to show their allegiance to and fit in with their peer group.

- to exclude others from their peer group, to show who is and is not part of the group.

- to control the behaviour of their peers.

Another factor of bullying is the emotional factor. The features of this are that they:

- may have been bullied in the past or currently.

- have feelings of insecurity and low self-esteem, so they bully to make themselves feel more powerful.

- do not understand other's emotions.
- don't know how to control their emotions, so they take out their feelings on other people.
- may not have the skills for handling social situations in healthy, positive ways.

The effect this had on me at the time was not realised until I was older and at that moment the overwhelming feeling of worthlessness nearly caused me to take a drastic, life changing direction. In my twenties I felt and most certainly was, suicidal. I suffered constant suicidal thoughts and idealisations. These manifested into a very dark day and one that nearly ended my life.

Sadly, whilst at school, there was no official action undertaken to prevent the bullying. I decided to do 2 things. First, I joined a local karate club and thought that it would help me if someone started bullying me, but soon realised that was not the right way to go. Reacting to violence with violence does not work. If anything, it increases the chances of the violence escalating.

The second thing I decided to do, was to act the fool. I decided to take on the persona of a 'Mr. Bean' type character. I thought if I made them laugh or make them see me as stupid then they would leave me alone. To my surprise, after a short period of time it worked. People laughed at me and instead of bullying me for my Deafness, they were asking me to 'play Mr. Bean'.

Being Deaf my language as is of other Deaf people, is made up of what we call Non-Manual Features (NMF). This means that the face and expressions shown on the face, replaces the intonation of the voice in a hearing person.

For example, as a hearing person your voice can reflect emotions, e.g., happy, sad, angry, frustrated, etc. As a Deaf person, we show these emotions in the way we sign but the visual clues are in the face.

By showing an angry face when signing, we can convey how angry we are by the intensity of both the signing and the facial expressions. Rowan Atkinson has this skill down to a fine art. His character Mr. Bean does not speak and only makes the odd vocalisation (Tedeee!). He manages to convey all his emotions in his facial expressions. You can see his moods and thinking by just looking at his posture and face.

My education from that point onwards, until I left at the age of 16 was manageable. There were the odd instances of bullying but overall, it was a lot less after I took on the image of a fool.

CHAPTER FOUR

FURTHER EDUCATION, FURTHER AGONY

"I imagine one of the reasons people cling to their hates so stubbornly is because they sense, once hate is gone, they will be forced to deal with the pain."

- James Baldwin

U p to the time when I left secondary education, I had improved greatly on the core subjects, Maths, Science, and English. The other subjects I took, I managed to get through, but it was still difficult as everything was conveyed through the CSW and the transference of the subject matter into BSL was demanding at best.

I was still in the process of learning BSL, and I did not have a 'complete' vocabulary at that time. My signing skills did improve as I went through the education system, including college.

I was reliant on skilled communication support workers (CSW's) who were good at their job, but unfortunately like all skills and jobs, some were better and more skilled than others. This caused extreme levels of frustration and stress. I would get irritated very easily when I could see my peers ploughing ahead in their knowledge acquisition, whilst I was 'bumbling' along behind. I felt on most days as though I was back at square one!

Having negative feelings throughout my school life was a miserable existence. I tried so hard to remain positive, but I felt overwhelmed by everything that I perceived, had gone wrong in my childhood.

Looking back, I realised that this was not having a good effect on my mental health and whilst writing this book and doing some research, I found some words that made clear sense to me.

"Think of anything positive to replace your negative thoughts. Instead of getting down about something, find something to be happy about and use this optimistic thought to replace the pessimistic thoughts. Practicing this over time, your mind will begin to focus on the good rather than the bad." (Anonymous)

At the time, I was not ready for these wise words. I was angry with the world, the people, and the school system I was stuck in. I was offered an opportunity to remain at the school and continue with 6th form. I had had enough of this and decided to opt out and head for College.

Because I had been at school in Hull, I decided to enrol on a College course. I signed up for an Art Course, but after 2 weeks I realised it was not what I really wanted and having to travel back and forth to Hull had started to grind me down. I had had this same journey for the last 6 years and I had had enough.

I decided to approach the SENCo at my school as they had told me when I left, that if I needed any advice or help, to get in touch. I explained that I was not happy at Hull and that the course I had signed up for wasn't working for me as well as I thought it would.

I did enjoy art and was quite successful at it, but I didn't see myself working in art in the future.

After a few phone calls by my SENCo, I was allowed to transfer to North Lindsey College in Scunthorpe. A visit was arranged, and an interpreter was provided for me, and I was interviewed and shown around the college site. After my visit I was accepted and signed up for a Foundation course in IT.

The course was for 1 year and it went well except for the Communication Support I was receiving. My SENCo had discussions with the college and explained that I needed BSL Interpreters with more course specific language skills. The college agreed and an interpreter was provided. I also had 2 more interpreters that were there for when my interpreter was unwell, on leave, etc. I had my 'main' interpreter with me for the next 4 years and this helped especially with continuity.

When I started the course, I bumped into a friend I hadn't seen since my first primary school aged 8. He had been a good friend and 'looked after' me when I was going through tough times.

When I was moved to Hull, he remained behind, and I never saw him again until I bumped into him one day on the college campus. We chatted and had lot of catching up to do.

We used to hang around together during the college day and see each other in the evenings on the odd occasions. We had managed to rebuild our initial friendship from many years before. We were just

16/17 years old, and our friendship became really strong. He seemed to recognise if I was struggling or having a bad time and was there for me always. Similarly, if he was having a tough time, I would be there to support him.

True friends are like that unlike some who say they are your friends but when things become difficult, they are nowhere to be seen. My college friend wasn't like that at all. We supported each other through thick and thin. We played football regularly and played on the same team and we had some amazing times together.

He was 1 year younger than me. So, when I met him at college, he would have been 17 years old. A year later when I was 19 my whole world was turned upside down when he died.

We used to play football together in a local park and on the day, he died we had arranged to meet up at the park.

We had been playing for a short time when my friend who was running after the ball, collapsed to the ground. I ran over and to see if he was okay. He was not breathing and fortunately, I had learnt basic First Aid when I was attending my Karate club.

I started resuscitation and was doing chest compressions and mouth to mouth while someone rang for an ambulance. After approximately 5 minutes, I could see that his lips had turned blue, and his skin was cold and pale. I knew he was dead and when the ambulance arrived, they confirmed it was too late.

I was terrified and blamed myself, believing that it was my fault that, he had died because I had not saved him.

I turned and ran. I ran and ran with no idea where to go. I was distraught, crying, and convincing myself that his death was my fault. I should have saved him. I did not return home for at least 5 hours and once home locked myself away in my bedroom. I didn't speak with anyone and constantly blamed myself for something that was obviously not my fault. At that time and with what had gone by since being a child, I was in a position where I was mentally vulnerable. I had not allowed anyone in, I refused to speak with anyone and left myself in a position where I was convinced everything was my fault.

Eventually it was explained to me that he had a heart condition that no one was aware of including himself. One moment he was fine and chatty and the next, he was gone…

It was a huge shock to everyone including myself and one from which I have never fully recovered. I am certain that this was the turning point in relation to the mental health issues I suffered.

I am sure that this event was the trigger that led me a few years later to consider taking my own life, to commit suicide.

The next year or so was incredibly tough for me and others. my mood changed; my attitude changed towards life in general. I was not a nice person to be around. I kept asking myself why, why, why?

I started to blame myself for his death. Looking back, I now realise that to think that, was irrational because, no one was to blame for an undetected heart complaint. But, as a teenager, you already have insecurities in everyday life.

We think nobody likes us. We believe the whole world is against us and everyone else is to blame. That is not true, but our perceptions tend to override our common sense unfortunately.

According to research:

(South West London and St. Georges Mental Health Trust NHS Fact Sheet)

'Suicide rates are higher for men than women of all age groups, and currently men are almost three times more likely than women to die by suicide. This gender gap has widened considerably over the past few decades. In the past, the ratio was 2:3 (Female/Male), the ratio is now 1:3. This means that three times more males are likely to commit suicide than females.'

'The gender difference in the suicide rate is particularly striking for young people. Between the ages of 20 and 24 years, men are more than four times more likely than women to kill themselves.' (NIMHE, 2007, National Suicide Prevention Strategy for England, Annual report on progress 2006.)

I struggled to keep my head above water after my friend's death. I was lethargic, I didn't care about things generally. Life didn't seem all that exciting back then.

I was not motivated and struggled to continue at college. I was lucky because I had my interpreter and other members of staff at the college who kept pushing me and encouraging me to carry on. If it wasn't for those people, I am not sure what would have happened.

Would I have been sat here writing this book? Would I have been working as a web developer and at the same time, run my own business. I don't believe I would have.

CHAPTER FIVE

THE LONELY YEARS

"Loneliness in not caused by others, it is when your mind tells you that nobody cares about you."

- Anonymous

Noreen Hertz in her book 'The Lonely Century' describes loneliness as being harmful. She goes onto explain that one study argued…

"That it's as bad for your health as smoking 15 cigarettes a day. When we are lonely, our heart rate goes up, our blood pressure rises and our cortisol levels, the levels in our bodies, go up. When loneliness is chronic, it increases the risk of serious illness, heart disease, and dementia."

What is the real definition of loneliness?

'Loneliness is the state of being alone and feeling sad about it. Your loneliness might lead you to sit at home listening to

depressing songs, or it could inspire you to go out and meet people… It's a feeling of sadness or even anxiety that occurs when you want company.' (www.vocabulary.com)

The irony of the quote is twofold. First it states loneliness might lead you to sit at home listening to depressing songs. For a profoundly Deaf person this means sitting and staring at four blank walls, in a room, alone, without company or support.

Secondly, it argues that it could lead you to go out and meet people. Here I was, a young Deaf man with no friends because my only friend had died. I couldn't communicate with the hearing people I was surrounded by, as my language was primarily BSL. Sadly, at the time and even today, I feel that some hearing people with no Deaf awareness, think of Deaf people as difficult to communicate with and even awkward. This pretty much summed up how I was feeling at the time. I foolishly, didn't seek support or help and didn't speak to my mother about it. Due to a lack of communication, from no outside professional support, my extended family had difficulty in communicating with me. This made me upset, and no doubt caused them to feel sad that they couldn't speak or communicate with me properly, and just relied on gestures.

I feel if basic BSL lessons were offered to close family members of a Deaf child it would increase not only basic communication levels, but support to build positive and trusting relationships to support that deaf child emotionally.

Is loneliness a disease? I have asked myself this question many times over the years. Loneliness is a universal human emotion that is both complex and unique to everyone. It has no single common cause, therefore the prevention and treatment of this potentially damaging state of mind can vary dramatically.

While common definitions of loneliness describe it as a state of solitude or being alone, loneliness is a state of mind. Loneliness causes people to feel empty, alone, and unwanted. People who are lonely often crave human contact but their state of mind makes it more difficult to form connections with other people. There are suggestions that loneliness is associated with social isolation, poor social skills, introversion, and depression. Loneliness, according to many experts, is not necessarily about being alone. Instead, if you feel alone and isolated, then that is how loneliness plays into your state of mind.

While research clearly shows that loneliness and isolation are bad for both mental and physical health, being alone is not the same as being lonely. In fact, solitude has several important mental health benefits, including allowing people to better focus and recharge.

Loneliness is marked by feelings of isolation despite wanting social connections. It is often perceived as an involuntary separation, rejection, or abandonment by other people. Solitude, on the other hand, is voluntary.

People who enjoy spending time by themselves continue to maintain positive social relationships that they can return to when they crave connection. They still spend time with others, but these interactions are balanced with periods of time alone. It is worth bearing in mind that loneliness is a state of mind linked to wanting human contact but feeling alone. People can be alone and not feel lonely, or they can have contact with people and still experience feelings of isolation.

I found it difficult from the ages of 17 to when I was around 23 years old and I think when looking back,

I was at my lowest point in relation to feeling lonely, depressed, miserable, and at a loss with what to do next.

I had managed somehow to get through the 4 years at college unscathed physically, mentally was a different matter. I achieved what it was I wanted to achieve. I had studied hard for 4 long years and acquired a good all-round knowledge of understanding and working within the field of IT.

The realisation at the end of the 4 years was, that I wanted to be a web developer. Initially, I had a period of unemployment which resulted in me being at home again, staring at 4 walls, heading in a downward spiral, into quite literally a pit of despair. Reading this will probably make you feel as though I am exaggerating but I truly felt like I was at rock bottom. To me at the age of 20, I thought I could not 'fall' any further. It was at that time when I started to experience darker thoughts. Thoughts that when I look back, horrify me. I remember vividly the feelings I had but when I do look back, I find myself in denial. Why did I disbelieve myself about how I felt? Perhaps because it seemed so ridiculous, my brain would not and will not accept that it could have been true.

Contributing factors to loneliness include things, such as physical isolation. The death of someone significant in a person's life can also lead to feelings of loneliness. Additionally, it can be a symptom of a psychological disorder such as depression. Depression often causes people to withdraw socially, which can lead to isolation. It can be said that loneliness can be a factor that contributes to symptoms of depression.

I had had a close, loyal friend die on me. That statement might sound selfish but that was how I felt at the time. Why me, why was it my friend who died, why didn't God choose someone else? I had had a shit life up until then. I had lived the first 16 years of my life with few friends and minimal language skills which were only useful within my small circle of Deaf friends.

Sixteen years of crap until I find a friend who accepted me for me and with whom I spent as much time as possible with for just over a year, then he's taken away from me. I fucking hated the world at the time. I offer no apology for the profanity used, I was an emotional mess. Now in my 30's I still feel bitter and sad about his demise. The difference now, with the benefit of time, is that I can manage it a lot better. My rebuilt mind has ensured that I have an emotional 'safety net' beneath me at all times. Is that a healthy thing or a bad thing? I honestly have no idea, but it works for me. How long it will stay with me I am not sure.

People who lack confidence in themselves often believe that they are unworthy of the attention or regard of other people, which can lead to isolation and chronic loneliness. Around my early 20's I did feel within myself unworthy. I blamed myself for the death of my friend. It must have been my fault. I'm the only friend who was with him the most. Perhaps my loneliness was contagious, and this is what made him unwell. So unwell that his heart couldn't cope and gave up on him. I suffered from low self-esteem. I was constantly feeling negative. I don't think I could count on one hand how many times I felt positive. It could be argued that personality factors may also play a role. Introverts, for example, might be less likely to cultivate and seek social connections, which can contribute to feelings of isolation and loneliness.

I see myself as an introvert rather than an extrovert. I am not the kind of person who enjoys mixing socially with large groups of people. I am usually the guy who stands at the back of the room or in the corner, keeping my head down, rather than being the centre of attention and being loud and lively. My self-confidence would never stretch to those levels. I'm happy standing back, watching and learning.

Looking back, I'm certain that my life was on hold. Nothing was happening for me that would motivate me to get up and get on with life. I gave my mother a pretty hard time, which to this day, I bitterly regret.

She was and still is the only person who understands where I am coming from.

As mentioned earlier, sourcing employment was practically impossible for me at the time, I felt that some employers were wary of employing me because of their lack of awareness and lack of knowledge about the support available - such as Deaf services and access to work schemes. However unfortunately, it depends on where you are based in regards to deaf services support, for example regions have different funding available to help. In the UK some regions offer employment support, support with benefits and bills etc but some regions have no funding for this and don't offer any of this support - this is something that needs to change.

At that time, there was a government scheme run by the Department of Work and Pensions (DWP). It was called the Access to Work (AtW) scheme. It was set up to enable people with either physical or mental health issues to get into paid employment. The scheme allowed the claimant to seek funding to pay for support in the workplace. As a Deaf person I was able to apply for a grant to pay for my communication support. This meant if I gained paid employment I could ask for an interpreter to be based alongside me to help with my English, phone calls, emails, translation of documents, including specification sheets for when developing a website. This did not come as a cost to the employer and therefore, was supposed to be an opportunity for equality in the workplace.

Sadly, for myself, this wasn't the case. I remember working for one company where I was physically and emotionally abused.

I clearly remember one time when I was working for a company that did web developing. I had been working beyond my contracted hours and often working until late evening to complete work that had been given to me. The other members of staff who were all hearing went home when they should have done, but my employer thought it was okay to force me to stay.

One evening it had got to around 10.00pm and I was both physically and mentally exhausted. I was hungry as I hadn't eaten since lunch and wanted to leave. As I tried to walk out of the office my employer grabbed me by the throat and threw me against the wall causing me to choke and leaving scratch marks on my neck. He screamed at me and pushed his fist close to my face. I managed to break free and walked off. It was so difficult to walk away. I wanted to turn back and punch him but I knew that was wrong and I would get into trouble. Arriving home my mother saw the injuries and asked me what on earth had happened. I stood in front of her and had to lie. I couldn't tell her what had really happened as she would have made me go to the police. I didn't want to lose my job, because I had worked so hard to get this job and waited for so long and I believe that in some companies employers were resistant to employ Deaf people - because of the lack of awareness and knowledge, so I was wary about returning to the job hunt again. I said I had been itching and scratched myself. Looking back, I'm not sure if she believed me and I haven't told her the truth even today. I'm not sure how she will feel if she reads this book. I continued to work for the same company for a little while more while looking for new employment elsewhere. The day I left wasn't a day too soon. It was a huge relief for me and I thought it would help me mentally to cope better.

CHAPTER SIX

WALKING FOR, AND WITH "L"

"I love walking in the rain because then no-one can see I'm crying."

- Anonymous

I was sitting around one day working on a website when an idea popped into my head, which, at the time, I didn't realise how much work it would take to organise. I decided to take part in a sponsored walk for my friend L, to raise money for relevant charities. He was and still is a friend who tragically lost his life quite a few years ago at a very young age. I decided I was going to walk from Scunthorpe to Cleethorpes for Mental Health and Suicide Awareness.

The walk was for me, a personal journey throughout. I have always thought of my friend since his passing and he is a constant reminder that life is too short and we should make the most of every day we walk and breathe.

I used to be like others when it came to life in general. If something didn't suit me I would quite easily have a moan about it and get angry. The difference is that I now also realise that I am lucky to have the opportunity to moan and groan. I've altered my attitude and take a more relaxed approach to situations that would have annoyed me and reacted negatively to.

The walk was going to be over 30 miles and was arranged for the end of August, hoping the weather was favourable on the day. With the assistance of my interpreter we set about contacting local organisations, companies, retail businesses asking for support. It was quite an eye opener as many came back to us with a negative response citing post Covid and the downfall in trade. Therefore, they felt they couldn't support us. We explained to them that this was to raise funds for Mental Health and Suicide Awareness, but this didn't work either.

We were fortunate that a few companies were brilliant and were generous with their donations and support. We contacted my local MP and received a positive response from them along with other people who were known to the media.

We decided to sit down and plan our intended route as being Deaf and my walking colleague being Deaf also, meant that the risk of traffic and possibility of getting injured was very high. Initially we spoke with the Police force who controlled the area we were walking through. When we explained what we were doing they advised us of how to ensure we remained safe throughout. We also informed the Road Traffic Officer about our upcoming charity walk and the route planned to ensure they were also aware too. They were astonished that we were going to walk that far and wished us well and encouraged us to take the right safety precautions. We did consider changing the timings of the walk but after much deliberation we decided to stick with the original plan and take on the advice and safety precautions from the Road Traffic Officers and Police. Several trips in the car driving the route and marking down where we were going to stop, where we needed vehicular support to protect us whilst walking along parts of the route and making sure we would be as safe as we could possibly be.

There were several 'photo' obligations to fulfil with sponsors and interviews conducted by local newspapers and local and national radio. These were of a huge benefit as they were able to put the word out through their own social media outlets and broadcasts, etc. From these, we were offered a little more support with things for example, refreshments and hi viz vests.

We had to decide where we were going to start from and we were lucky to be allowed to start from the local golf club Forest Pines. We knew we would be finishing our walk on the Pier in Cleethorpes 30 miles later. It was decided we would leave the golf course at 07.00am and hopefully be in Cleethorpes before 17.00pm.

As the day got closer, we had a few things to sort out and my walking colleague informed me that he was having an issue with his knee. He wasn't going to pull out and managed the walk using 2 walking poles.

We contacted the police again to inform them how we were going to ensure our safety and they seemed a little more relaxed and would try and do the odd 'drive by' to ensure all was well.

After an early night for all of us, the next morning we stood in the car park of Forest Pines at 06.30am wondering what on earth were we thinking of. Anyway, it was too late to change our minds. After grabbing a welcome cup of coffee we set out and headed towards the local village of Scawby and then onto Brigg following the back roads for safety. As we approached Brigg, I realised the 'new' trainers I had bought especially for the walk were not as comfortable as I thought they would be, so a quick change into an old pair I had with me and a change of socks was called for.

The next stretch was tough and uphill a lot of the way, so after putting a fresh pair of socks on and some refreshments we were ready to head towards our next stopping point.

Overall, it took us just over 10 hours to get to our destination and a well-earned drink and rest. I remember walking onto the beach and going down on one knee and pointing to the sky in memory of my friend L. I felt he was with me all the way during the walk. He was the third person on the walk besides my friend and I.

Mentally it had a twofold effect on me. Firstly, it was an emotional experience and I felt he was whispering words of encouragement during the tougher parts of the walk and pushing me on towards the finish line. Secondly it was an overwhelming relief that we had done it. It had taken 4-5 months of hard work, hundreds of e-mails, hundreds of phone calls but we achieved our goal. A local community project benefited from a much-needed donation too.

Looking back on this I discovered new things, things that I had not known about before. Mental health includes our emotional, psychological, and social well-being. It affects how we think, feel, and act as we cope with life. It also helps determine how we handle stress, relate to others, and make choices.

Mental health issues can affect your thinking, mood, and behaviour. Your mental health can also affect your physical health. Therefore, when I was younger and started to recognise that I might have 'issues' I joined a gym.

I also started doing exercises indoors and running outdoors over varying distances. Now I am running 3-4 times a week to help me 'free' myself of stress related issues. It helps me to totally clear my mind and breathes a new life into me. I know that sounds a little dramatic, but it is exactly how I feel when I am running. Sometimes if things are going badly for me I will run up to 11 miles in one session. I am not a fast runner. I like to take my time, look around at my surroundings and cleanse my mind of all external influences.

Good Mental Health, according to the World Health Organisation (WHO) is defined as a state of well-being where individuals are able to:

- Realise their own potential
- Work productively
- Cope with the normal stresses of life
- Make a positive contribution to the community

Mental and psychological well-being encompasses the way you feel about yourself, but also the way you deal with outside influences and the quality of your relationships. It's important to remember that positive mental health is not the absence of mental health issues, such as depression or anxiety. Being mentally healthy is mainly about the presence of positive aspects such as a feeling of purpose, contentment, maintaining fulfilling relationships and participating in life to the max.

Positive mental health allows you to enjoy all the activities you want to be involved in. It doesn't mean you will never be sad or go through emotionally challenging times. However, I believe those with positive mental health will be able to bounce back more easily from these experiences. I have found this to be the case on many occasions.

I try to remain focused on the positives and disregard the negatives as best as possible. I may not achieve that every time, but I try to ensure if I do have those 'dark moments' they are short lived rather than become prolonged, drawn-out episodes.

CHAPTER SEVEN

MY HEROES

"My hero is an ordinary person who finds strength to persevere and endure in spite of overwhelming obstacles."

- Carol Adamski

My Roadmap to Positivity. Throughout History, role-models have played a crucial role in helping to abolish discrimination against specific groups of people. *Rosa Parks, Harvey Milk, Martin Luther King Jr, Emmeline Pankhurst, and Nelson Mandela* are a few examples of role models who have been at the forefront of the fight to end discrimination and stigma.

Today we have the same stigma and discrimination. People are currently being discriminated against on account of mental illness, in society and in the workplace. There is also a stigma which is preventing people from talking about mental ill-health and sometimes, seeking the help that they need.

We need role models to break this down. True role models are those who possess the qualities that we would like to have and those who have affected us in a way that makes us want to be better people. They help us to advocate for ourselves and take a leadership position on the issues that we believe in.

Whilst researching this book and looking at role models I came across an interesting article written by *Cayenne Consulting* a company based in California. They have written an article describing the 7 traits of a role model and I would like to share this with you the reader. I thought the traits that are identified offer an excellent definition of a role model.

Demonstrate confidence and leadership.

A good role model is always positive, calm, and confident in themselves. You don't want someone who is down or tries to bring you down. Everyone likes a person who is happy with their achievements but continues to strive for bigger and better objectives.

Don't be afraid to be unique.

Whatever you choose to do with your life, be proud of the person you've become, even if that means accepting some ridicule. You want role models who won't pretend to be someone they are not and won't be fake just to suit other people.

Communicate and interact with everyone.

Good communication means listening as well as talking. People are energized by leaders who explain why and where they are going.

Great role models know they must have a consistent message and business plan, and repeat it repeatedly until everyone understands.

1. Show respect and concern for others. You may be driven, successful and smart, but whether you choose to show respect or not speaks volumes about how other people see you. Everyone notices if you are taking people for granted, not showing gratitude, or stepping on others to get ahead.

2. Be knowledgeable and well rounded. Great role models aren't just "teachers." They are constant learners, challenge themselves to get out of their comfort zones, and surround themselves with

smarter people. When team members see that their role model can be many things, they will learn to stretch themselves to be successful.

3. Have humility and willingness to admit mistakes. Nobody is perfect. When you make a bad decision, let those who are watching and learning from you know that you made a mistake and how you plan to correct it. By apologising, accepting accountability and correcting course, you will be demonstrating an often-overlooked part of being a role model.

4. Do good things outside the job. People who do the work, yet find time for good causes outside of work, such as raising money for charity, saving lives, and helping people in need get extra credit. Commitment to a good cause implies a strong commitment to the business.

True role models are those who possess the qualities that we would like to have, and those who have affected us in a way that makes us want to be better people. They help us to advocate for ourselves and take a more defined position on the issues that we believe in.

One of my role models from my earlier years and one of my 'heroes' was the England player David Beckham. He set himself very high standards and tried to represent what people should be expected to behave like in everyday life. He was seen as a leader of men both on and off the pitch. He was awarded the captains armband for England as he was a natural leader and showed good leadership.

He was a person that never gave up and was persistent in everything he did. An excellent example of not giving up when the pressure is on was when England played Greece in a World Cup qualifier. England needed a goal to go through to the world cup finals. England were awarded a free kick and Beckham stepped up, placed the ball, and took the kick. The fans were distraught because he missed. English fans expected him to score.

Later in the game we (England) were awarded a second free kick. David Beckham placed the ball and told others who were interested to walk away. He stepped back, moved forward, and kicked the ball. It flew towards the goal and missed. The English fans were disappointed for a second time. At the very end of the game England was awarded a third free kick. Up stepped Beckham and took hold of the ball. Players surrounded him and suggested that the captain ought to give someone else a go as we desperately needed a goal, otherwise our world cup was over. Fans were yelling and screaming for someone else to take the kick. David Beckham stood there in front of 90,000 loyal fans who were baying for blood. Millions of others around the country were staring him down. He placed the ball, stepped back, and closed his eyes. Blocking out all the sounds coming from the crowd, he breathed in slowly, held his breath and put his boot through the ball and watched, as in slow motion, the ball sail away and head towards goal. Everyone was holding their breath, some couldn't look and turned their backs or closed their eyes. The ball curled in mid-air and went into the top left-hand corner of the goal, beating the flaying arms of the Greek goalkeeper.

The ground erupted as did the country and Beckham had done it. He had ensured England's place in the World Cup finals. It would have been very easy for him to give the ball to another player. He could have walked away from the pressure cooker moment, but David being David, decided that he would take ownership, knowing if he missed, then the whole country would blame him, leaving the rest of the team 'verbally' unscathed.

David Beckham demonstrated confidence and leadership. He showed he was not afraid of being unique, knowing that if he missed, he would face ridicule.

He showed that he was able to communicate and interact with his fellow team-mates demonstrating that he could talk and listen to others at the same time. He showed respect and concern for others. He knew the whole country was relying on him to lead and be successful. This he showed by scoring the goal that put England through. He was knowledgeable and well rounded, he demonstrated that he wasn't frightened to step outside his comfort zone to achieve whatever it was that was needed, i.e., a goal.

David had humility and willingly accepted his mistakes. He had missed two free kicks and the third one was right at the end of the game. The pressure was incredible, he had millions of people yelling, screaming and imploring him to give someone else a chance. His name and the goal were recorded as one of the greatest moments for an England football captain.

He was a natural leader and respected by all. Therefore, David Beckham is one of my heroes. I'd like to think, that if I was in a pressure situation, I wouldn't back away. If anything, I would put my best foot forward and 'have a go'.

Bruce Lee, the famous Martial Arts expert, and film star is another of my heroes. Sadly, he passed away at the age of 32. Ironically, he died of a brain inflammation apparently caused by a headache remedy. For someone who was incredibly fit, it seemed a strange way to die. There was a lot of suspicion and speculation to how he died but his death certificate records his death as brain swelling.

He had through his teachings and philosophical outlook on life installed an attitude of positiveness inside of me. He had died before I had heard his name but, through films and books I began to see how he believed life should be lived. One of his quotes that I remember is,

"Defeat is a state of mind; No one is ever defeated until defeat has been accepted as a reality"

His belief was that you should lead your life in a positive manner. You should not accept failure until all other options are wasted. Do not give up, if one method fails, then try another and keep trying until you are successful.

Lee also believed that your inner strength defines a person. He believed that life is in a constant change, and unless we learn to adapt to it we're bound to experience tremendous resistance that will entrap us in a state of suffering.

Lee likened the person who embraced change to water. People tend to see water as a weakness, but Lee disagreed, he regarded water as the ultimate symbol of strength and came up with one of his famous quotes:

"Be like water because it is soft, resilient, and formless. It can never be snapped."

Another of his most famous quotes is:

"Always be yourself, express yourself, have faith in yourself, do not go out and look for a successful personality and duplicate it."

I have always tried to follow this 'rule' of life. I have always been myself and tried to believe in the things that I do. If I have made mistakes, I go back over them and try to see what went wrong, then try to ensure if the opportunity arises again in the future, I do it differently, hence learning from my mistakes.

Bruce Lee also said:

"Mistakes are always forgivable, if one has the courage to admit them."

I have made sure that I do not copy another person's beliefs and lifestyle. I will observe and take onboard what they say or feel and may even, adopt a part of that for myself. I feel it is important to be your own person, to follow your own path. To ensure that you are constantly prepared to adapt. I guess it is akin to Bruce Lee's philosophy and relationship and the notion of water being the ultimate strength. Every single person is unique. A lot of people do not embrace this uniqueness, instead they try to be something different. Perhaps it is out of fear or that they are trying to emulate their hero. Bruce Lee points out in an essay he wrote in 1973:

"Most people only live for their image. That is why where some have a self, a starting point, most people have a void. Because they are so busy projecting themselves as "this" or "that," they end up wasting and dissipating all their energy in projection

and conjuring up of a facade, rather than centring their energy on expanding and broadening their potential or expressing and relaying this unified energy for efficient communication."

According to Bruce, to follow your inner voice and honestly express yourself is a prerequisite for self-discovery and personal growth. In his own words:

"In life, what more can you ask for than to be real? To fulfil one's potential instead of wasting energy on [attempting to] actualise one's dissipating image, which is not real and an expenditure of one's vital energy. We have great work ahead of us, and it needs devotion and much, much energy. To grow, to discover, we need involvement, which is something I experience every day - sometimes good, sometimes frustrating. No matter what, you must let your inner light guide you out of the darkness."

Mark 'Billy' Billingham is someone I admire and is a hero because of his self-belief and his positive attitude towards life in general. He served as a member of the Parachute Regiment for 9 years and then applied for selection to the Special Air Service. He was successful and during his 17 years' service, rose to one of the highest ranks in the Regiment. He rose to the Rank of Regimental Sergeant Major, Warrant Officer First Class.

He led teams throughout the world and excelled in every area of service he applied himself to. On several occasions he could have been killed, but through luck and tenacity he survived to tell his tale.

As a young boy living near Birmingham he had become involved with a local gang and on one occasion when fighting with members of a different gang he was stabbed in the back, missing his kidney by millimetres. He was rushed to hospital and whilst there, a doctor told him, if he had lost any more blood he would have died. This was his 'wake-up' call and from that point he decided he needed to 'sort' out his life and lifestyle.

He never gave up on a venture and never perceived quitting anything he applied himself to.

He was a fighter and always backed his fellow colleague's 100 percent of the time. After he left the SAS he decided to go down the route of a bodyguard and worked for and with some of Hollywood's well-known stars, including Tom Cruise, Brad Pitt, Angelina Jolie and their 6 children. He also worked with and alongside Sean Penn.

His next venture was to work with and build a charity in Haiti. He did this alongside Sean Penn and others and today the charity is growing day by day and assists and helps people who are at their lowest point in life. He has a motto that he is known to use on many occasions. *Always a little further* is Mark's philosophy on life. He believes that when you feel as though you are at your limit, it is better if you try and go *"Always a little further"*. With this philosophy in life I believe that when I am at a point where I cannot go any further, I tell myself *'Always go a little further'*. This pushes my limits beyond what I thought was impossible. It makes me feel better as I have achieved more than was expected of me. It makes me feel more positive and it has helped me to *'Rebuild my mind'*.

Jason 'foxy' Fox is another of my heroes who I admire for his endurance and never say never attitude. He was a former member of the Royal Marines and Special Boat Service (SBS). He was medically discharged in 2012 suffering and being diagnosed as having PTSD.

What followed for him, was years of loneliness and despair, trying to fight his demons whilst suffering with his Mental Health. This nearly took him to the brink as he contemplated suicide but managed to step back from the precipice and challenged himself to get through to the *'other side'*. He now presents alongside other colleagues, the Channel 4 show SAS Who Dares Wins.

In 2011 he was assigned the role of Team Leader and was responsible for leading a team of Special Forces (SF) soldiers on a 6-month tour, but he was feeling despondent. He described in his own words,

"The tour was like a black cloud looming towards me."

"I wasn't looking forward to going away and that was the first time I'd ever felt like that. I was losing my military mojo."

He approached the camps mental health nurse and explained how he was feeling and was eventually diagnosed with PTSD. He felt his life was over. If he couldn't be Special Forces then why bother with anything else. He didn't believe he was suffering from PTSD and thought he was going to be fine. Shortly after, his home life started to deteriorate, and he then headed in a downward spiral of severe depression.

Living in Devon, he wasn't having much luck with therapists and therapy and was trapped in a downward spiral of negativity. One day he found himself standing on a clifftop contemplating suicide. he described the situation as:

"Whether I was gonna jump or not, I don't know."

"But I think that moment needed to happen. I needed to be standing there contemplating that maybe the best thing for me was to kill myself. Because I was like, 'Right, hang on a minute. I either jump or I change something about how I do stuff.' I changed my life hugely after that point."

Looking back at myself in my early 20's, I was in the same situation. At that time a lot was happening in my life. I had lost my best friend when I was 19. I had continued with my college education until I was 20. Around that time, all my friends who had grown up together decided to leave my hometown and move on. They cited the death of my friend as the reason and poor employment opportunities. I had been to the Job centre many times, trying to source employment unsuccessfully.

This made me become more depressed and I was fearful that I would never get a job. My family tried to be encouraging in my job hunt, without realising the difficulties that I faced. This didn't help me as it made me feel worse about myself. I was desperate to get a job. I was fed up with being stuck at home, staring at 4 walls and no social contact at all besides my own mother.

Eventually I managed to get a 2-week work trial at a well-known car company. The job was for a valet, and part of my role was to make sure the cars for sale looked clean. After the 2-week trial I was offered the job but at the time I was receiving a fair amount of verbal abuse from the senior manager. I tried to ignore this and carried on with my job. About 3 weeks into the job the same manager approached me and told me to pick up a car engine and throw it in the skip.

This was a full engine, and it was impossible to pick up on my own. After several attempts I told him I couldn't lift it. He was furious with me and started to scream at me and was being abusive.

I went home and explained to my mum what had happened, she was understandably upset for me and she suggested I go back to the job centre and explain what happened. When I returned to the job centre, they had managed to find a BSL Interpreter for me. I explained what had happened and they said it was clearly discriminatory and that I should raise a discrimination case against the garage and its owners. Unfortunately, a short while after this happened, the company declared themselves bankrupt and sold the business. For a further period I was unemployed again.

As part of the job seeking rules I was required to continue searching for work and applying for interviews.

This went on for nearly a year after losing my job as a valet. I was feeling more despondent by the day. My routine was the same day in day out, week after week, month after month.

Shortly before everything came to a head, I lost my grandmother who sadly passed away at the age of 85. I was really close to her and she kind of 'got me'. It was nice for the both of us to spend time together, I always remember her asking me to help clean her windows because I was so much taller than her, it's nice memories like this that I continue to treasure.

On the actual morning, I think it was at the weekend, I woke up and after mulling things over in my mind I jumped in my car and drove to the Peak District. During the journey my head was swirling around and around. I was in turmoil and felt total despair. I was at the point of "fuck it, life is not worth it anymore". I felt I had nothing to lose. I didn't have any friends, I didn't have a job, I was lonely, feeling isolated and decided enough was enough.

I arrived and parked my car and got out and left my keys in the ignition. I had decided at that point, that I wasn't coming back. This was my final 'journey' and therefore, didn't need a car to get back home because I wasn't going home. I was going to walk and walk until I found a place to end my life and quite simply, die.

Leaving the car, I headed off and later found myself on top of a cliff. Looking down, I suddenly thought, it would be so easy to take one more step and walk off the cliff. The drop below would have easily been enough to kill me. It was a strange feeling. One of almost peace and serenity. All my worries from the past could be eradicated in a matter of seconds. It would have been painless apart from the millisecond after impact on the ground below. I stood there stock still, looked around and had a question swimming around inside my head.

"Do I go for it and step into the void, or do I step back, walk away and try to turn my life around?"

As I stood there teetering on the edge, rocking slowly back and forth, an image of my mother appeared in my head and the agony she would suffer, having to bury her only child. I felt a huge lump in my throat and an enormous amount of guilt. Jumping would be an incredibly selfish thing to do. My mother didn't deserve this at all. I stood there motionless for what must have seemed an age.

The first thing I realised, was that you've got to admit things to yourself before you go and try to fix them. What I soon realised was, that you can't change the past, but you can certainly try to change the future. This was the defining moment when I decided I was going to be a new person with a rebuilt mind.

Stepping back from the edge, I turned around and started the long walk back to my car. I felt alive, a feeling of exhilaration surged through me. When I sat in the car, I punched the steering wheel several times resulting in damaging my knuckles. I screamed out loud.

I had a very long drive to get back home which helped provide me with time to think. I re-ran the earlier part of the day through my mind and wondered what the hell I was thinking. It was a selfish act in my opinion and not planned at all.

Once I arrived home I kicked of my shoes and went into the kitchen and drank lots of water. I then sat down and decided to create a mind map which would help direct me towards getting out of this negative mood and change and move into a positive mindset. It took me about 2 hours and once I had set everything out it made things a lot clearer for me. It was time to drag myself out of my pit of despair and step up and challenge myself to change. It was going to be the biggest challenge of my life to date. I literally pressed CTRL+ALT+DEL I needed to reset my brain like I would reset a computer.

I stopped going to the local pub and clubs. I didn't drink for over a year and started eating a lot healthier. My thought was, if I had a healthy body that would lead to a healthy mind.

I was literally ready to commit suicide without a thought or worry for others. I thought suicide was a simple process but I discovered how wrong I was. Suicide is a complex subject and many have tried to explain the thought process behind it.

While researchers say most suicides are more impulsive, some people leave behind an obvious trail. People who are feeling helpless, carrying blame, putting their affairs in order, giving away possessions. With all those things happening, we sometimes do not see it at the time.

Despite all the research, there still isn't a proven formula that can predict precisely who is going to kill themselves and who won't, which interventions work for all, or work for a while, and which don't. Certain words might save someone one day only to have them slip away the next. It doesn't make any sense why one person who demonstrates all the risk factors lives and another kills themselves. The only person who can explain is gone.

Looking at suicide in general, there are many factors or triggers that might activate thoughts of suicide. This does not mean that they will be acted out. It could be argued that many of us have suicidal thoughts and the ending of life. For most people this will be a fleeting thought, for others it will be a constant that needs to be addressed as quickly as possible. Intervention is a priority.

The question is, why and where do these thoughts arise from?

Some of the following signs that demonstrate a 'path' towards feeling suicidal are:

- feeling or appearing to feel trapped or hopeless
- having mood shifts, either happy or sad
- experiencing agitation or a heightened state of anxiety
- experiencing changes in personality, routine, or sleep patterns
- getting their affairs in order and giving things away
- experiencing depression, panic attacks, or impaired concentration
- isolating themselves
- talking about being a burden to others
- experiencing psychomotor agitation such as pacing or wringing the hands
- saying goodbye to others as though it were the last time

- experiencing a loss of enjoyment in previously pleasurable activities, such as eating, exercise, social interaction, or sex
- expressing severe remorse and self-criticism
- talking about suicide or dying
- expressing regret about being alive or ever having been born *(various sources)*

For me it was a mixture of things. My mind felt tormented and random thoughts were spinning around inside my head. I wanted to hit my head against the wall to try and stop my head churning. At the time I was contemplating taking my life, I was constantly agitated. I was angry with society and the world. I hated myself so much, I became fixated on the anger and was at a point where I thought I was going to implode. I became isolated from others and paranoid about everything and everyone. My trust in others was non-existent.

Paranoia is defined as:

"An extreme and unreasonable feeling that other people do not like you or are going to harm or criticise you." (Cambridge Dictionary)

Or:

"a tendency on the part of an individual or group toward excessive or irrational suspiciousness and distrustfulness of others" (Merriam Webster Dictionary)

I had very little faith or trust in others, including my mother at that time. I was convinced that my friends had all left because of me. I blamed myself for the death of my friend years earlier which looking back was totally irrational. I had no idea he was unwell. I was asking for help from many people and wasn't receiving anything back.

CHAPTER EIGHT

LIVING ON THE HAMSTER WHEEL OF LIFE!

"Have you ever just looked at someone and knew the wheel was turning but the hamster was dead."

- Anonymous

The pursuit of happiness for me, was like running on a treadmill - no matter how fast I ran, I could never catch it.

Plato approached happiness as a form of personal growth - *it's about getting satisfaction from our achievements, not from what those accomplishments can earn us.*

As Aristotle said, *"Happiness depends upon ourselves."*

Gustavo Razzetti (March 18th 2019) said:

"Happiness is relative. It's neither a gift other people give to us nor something that things provide us. Happiness is something we create from within."

The word 'happiness' wasn't a word I recognised when I was at my lowest point in life. No matter how hard I tried, I could not create an ounce of happiness for myself. Everyone around me thought all was well and I was enjoying life to the max but, this was just a facade.

I was a total fake and when I looked in the mirror, I did not recognise the face staring back at me. I was scared and frightened. I could not, at the time, understand how I had turned into the person I had become.

I guess happiness was a concept that floated around in the back of my mind but at the forefront was despair.

Despair appeared in many forms for me. Despair was my best friend. It sounds a little desperate to state that, but, to me it was a reality. Despair dined at the head of the table, it slept with me like a lover and awoke with me like my worst enemy.

I came to both hate and embrace despair on many occasions.

It seemed that my life was going to be a continuous rollercoaster of emotions and agonies. It was all consuming and ate away slowly at my mind and spirit. It dominated everything I wanted to do. It was numero uno.

Looking back, I wondered how I ever managed to drag myself out of a pit of misery and drag myself into the life I enjoy now.

Despair was like a drug that I was hooked on and ever reliant on. It was an unforgettable period in my life and is a constant reminder of how bad things really were.

It reminded me of a verse by Joe Fazio:

"While happiness is the twin sibling of despair, it is despair that is the stronger of the two."

"In life. happiness are but fleeting moments. Despair lurks forever in the shadows of our mind and our hearts...until the final darkness."

When you are struggling under the weight of despair, simple tasks feel overwhelming, getting out of bed, taking a shower, or leaving the house. To live with despair means waking up with a heavy load on your chest, and a feeling of exhaustion, no matter how many hours you have slept.

You see problems as insurmountable for example, grieving the loss of a loved one or, a dear and close friend.

I wish I could say I have resolved the despair I had felt, but the truth is, I have had to learn to live with it. No happy ending lasts forever.

Deep despair has a sinister, punishing quality. To regain your footing is to go into battle with your most brutal demons. Though once the battle is over, you still, may not be able to resolve the problems that you have faced.

CHAPTER NINE

TAKE YOUR DESPAIR FOR A WALK

"People may not realize this, but it's sadness and despair that sometimes allow a person to grow. Being comfortable with where you're at often doesn't motivate you to change or improve your situation. However, being in despair forces you to try to get out of it. That's why despair is a good thing."

- Anonymous

Once a day, try your best to get out of the house for some fresh air. A brisk walk raises your metabolism, boosts endorphins, and will give you much-needed headspace. Shaking off tension and gaining some vitamin D can also offer some relief. I put a lot of faith in the below points, these really helped me through tough times.

1. Honour your despair.

Please don't deny it. Don't push it away. When you acknowledge your despair, you take away some of its power over you.

2. Seek out fellowship.

Isolation fuels despair. Seek out the company of people who share your experience.

3. Avoid toxic positivity.

Such phrases, like *"Everything happens for a reason,"* are insensitive to those who are truly suffering. Toxic positivity from others feels insulting when you're faced with difficulties and despair.

Despair may knock the wind out of you, but when embraced and managed effectively, it can also lift you to even greater heights.

It can be said that the opposite of despair is hope. Hope is seen as an association with an expectation and a desire for something to happen. It can be said that when we hope we are essentially concentrating on a result of some sorts.

And, if that result doesn't occur, then we may fall into despair, which is the lack of the expectation and desire for a certain thing to happen.

We cannot have hope without despair. They go hand in hand like night and day. If you can feel hope then you most certainly, can feel despair.

Despair can be destroying and drains all your energy. I know that appears to be a drastic comment, but I firmly believed it at the time and still do now albeit less. It has been true in my own experience.

I believe there are two forms of anger: uncontrolled anger, and controlled anger.

Anger in any form, gets your heart pumping, and makes you want to do something, and not just be dragged under.

I used to sit at home day in day out, staring at four walls until one day I thought 'fuck it' and decided to go to a local gym. Running, pushing weights, and swimming would instantly make me feel in control of my emotions and would help me see beyond my despair and anger. This was my way of grasping the idea of controlled anger.

At the time I felt I needed something more than the exercise at my local gym. I discovered through watching television, the sport of MMA. Mixed martial arts were, I thought, a way of releasing the uncontrolled anger that was bubbling away inside of me. I felt like a volcano that was about to explode.

I found a place where they ran MMA lessons and signed up and to be honest, enjoyed the sport, I had a couple of contested fights and as par for the sport, picked up a few injuries along the way.

After a period, I realised this was not the way to control or 'tame' my frustration and anger. I withdrew from the MMA sport and concentrated on my Karate. Karate for me was another way to control my 'inner self' and it helped my body be in tune with my brain and vice versa.

Karate is a Japanese martial art whose physical aspects seek the development of defensive and counterattacking body movements.

The themes of traditional karate training are fighting and self-defence, though its mental and moral aspects target the overall improvement of the individual. This is facilitated by the discipline and persistent effort required in training.

For me, it was all about learning and taking onboard, self-discipline. It was my release from frustration and loneliness every week. It was something that I truly engaged with and during my period of learning I achieved my Black belt and the skills learnt, made me think more positively. I started to see a tiny light at the end of a very long, dark, tunnel.

Looking back, I think the aggressiveness that was channelled through the gym, the MMA ring, and Karate, helped me to realise that there were ways of controlling myself and to start to believe in a more positive, open minded outlook on life.

The Collins COBUILD dictionary defines 'Doom' as:

"A terrible future state or event which you cannot prevent."

It is, what I believe, a situation I found myself in, I was in a position whereby I thought that my life had nowhere to go. To me, I personally felt that there was no future to look forward to. My past had been a painful one and I was in the position where I had had enough, and I didn't see any hope for the future.

I felt that I couldn't control what was happening around my everyday life. I was also unable to make decisions clearly as I was constantly consumed by negativity, I was so angry with society and life.

I knew that to drag myself from this situation would need huge amounts of effort and energy. I had to start thinking positively. I had to establish a mindset whereby I was applying positive thinking rather than negative thinking.

CHAPTER TEN

POSITIVE THINKING

"Look for something positive in every day, even if some days you have to look a little harder."

\- Unknown

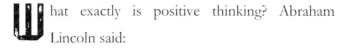hat exactly is positive thinking? Abraham Lincoln said:

"Most folks are as happy as they make up their minds to be."

What is exactly positive thinking? You might think it is seeing the world through rose tinted spectacles or glossing over the negative aspects of life.

However, positive thinking is taking on the negative things in life and the challenges that occur with a positive outlook. Positive thinking does not necessarily mean avoiding or ignoring the bad things; instead, it involves making the most of the potentially bad situations, trying to see the best in other people and viewing yourself and your abilities in a positive light. This was the path I was trying to go down after my period of despair and hopelessness. After I had turned away from the cliff edge and walked back to my car I had decided that I needed to change my outlook on life.

I was aware that changing my approach was not going to be straightforward. It took a tremendous amount of willpower and determination on my part to change from an absolute negative outlook on life and everyone, to a more positive, hopeful way to move forward in my life and in everyday things that I was going to do.

Whilst reading and researching the area of positive thinking I came upon some amazing positive thinking quotes, which I would like to share here with you.

"No one stays with you permanently, so learn to survive alone." (Anon)

"Sometimes you have to just turn the page to realise there's more to your book of life than the page you're stuck on. Don't try to fix what's been broken in your past, let your future create something better." (Anon)

And finally, for now…

"Keeping one's attitude positive, especially when the world conspires to make us mad, is one of the greatest accomplishments of life." (Brendon Burchard)

CHAPTER ELEVEN

NO F*CKING SOCIAL MEDIA

"When social media becomes a place where you start to share your negative thoughts or you become negative from other people's posts, remove yourself before you ruin your reputation."

\- Anonymous

The activity of scrolling and searching for bad news even though it's disheartening, is often referred to as 'doom-scrolling'. An activity that has risen in popularity as we seem to navigate disaster after disaster. In my earlier days of using social media incessantly, I was a doom-scroller.

Doom-scrolling is not a harmless activity. It is a disease and is an addiction that I did not need. Every day I was bouncing back and forth between various social media platforms. I was gorging myself on the rubbish, I can say rubbish because the majority of what

I read coming from both the hearing and Deaf community was utter garbage. I was devouring this garbage day in, day out. It was an obsession I was unable to control. Each day I was being dragged slowly down into another pit of despair.

So why do we do it? At its core, doom-scrolling is a totally human reaction to what we're going through. When stressful things are happening in our life our primitive brain takes over and is concerned with keeping us alive above all else. This can lead to us scanning for danger, putting ourselves on high alert for anything that could be perceived as a threat.

In my eyes I believed that I was surrounded by unwanted threats. I became paranoid about anything I was told or saw. To me, life was one huge conspiracy and the majority of that was via doom-scrolling.

Of course news outlets don't help matters with constant coverage and sensationalist headlines. When people then take to social media, perhaps reporting inaccurate news or making inflammatory comments, it adds fuel to the fire. So it's no wonder that when we go online it feels like the world is burning sometimes.

We know this response is a perfectly natural and human one but that doesn't mean we should feed into it. If you're finding yourself getting sucked into this kind of behaviour, it's time to get more intentional with your online habits.

I decided to go down the radical route and remove myself from all social media - for personal accounts only and to continue to only have access to social media accounts linked to my business and motivational speeches. Around the same time I was also experiencing some problems with some 'friends', who were also Deaf, so this unfortunately made me become distant from the Deaf community. I felt at the time that it was my only choice due to the problems I was having and wanted to protect myself. I am lucky enough that now I have some wonderful people I call friends from the Deaf community.

Doom-scrolling is often a 'mindless' habit. We're being led by fear when we're doing it, often time and place just slips away as we're sucked into whatever's happening. Embracing mindfulness and checking in with how we're feeling more often can only be a good thing. Ask yourself how is everything, how is your day going, what can you do to make the situation better? In turn, try and offer a solution or answer to each question you ask. If you cannot find a suitable answer then make sure you take note, when you 'check in' again later ask yourself the same question and ensure you have an answer this time. Mindfulness is paramount to make this succeed. The definition of mindfulness is:

"A mental state achieved by focusing one's awareness on the present moment, while calmly acknowledging and accepting one's feelings, thoughts and bodily sensations, used as a therapeutic technique."

Mindfulness is a straightforward word. It suggests that the mind is fully attending to what's happening, to what you're doing, to the space you're moving through. That might seem trivial, except for the annoying fact that we so often veer from the matter at hand. Our mind takes flight, we lose touch with our body and soon we're engrossed in obsessive thoughts about something that just happened or fretting about the future; that makes us anxious. Mindfulness is the basic human ability to be fully present, aware of where we are and what we're doing and not overly reactive or overwhelmed by what's going on around us.

Mindfulness is a quality that every human being already possesses, it's not something you have to conjure up, you just have to learn how to access it.

To exercise the value of mindfulness you need to find time and step off the hamster wheel of life. You need to find opportunities or deliberately set aside some *'you time'*. Mindfulness is a simple, basic, necessity of *'normal'* everyday living and it should be a given.

Mindfulness means many things:

"Mindfulness isn't difficult. We just need to remember to do it." (Sharon Salzburg)

"Mindfulness is a way of befriending ourselves and our own experience."

"Life is a dance. Mindfulness is witnessing that dance."

"Mindfulness is the aware, balanced acceptance of the present experience. It isn't more complicated than that. It is opening to or receiving the present moment, pleasant or unpleasant, just as it is, without clinging to it or rejecting it." (Eckhart Tolle)

Mindfulness appears to be a simple, straightforward concept, which is easily mastered. On the contrary, it is extremely difficult to access. Mindfulness entails trying to get the mind to look at the mind. Albert Einstein proposed:

"You cannot solve a problem from the same consciousness that created it."

Our brains are like a highly sophisticated spaceship flying across a very hectic universe at the speed of light, our brains most of the time are on autopilot.

Mindfulness can help us 're-boot' our hard drive, reinvigorate our brains, akin to a CTRL+ALT+DEL.

Doing some research for this topic, I found three reasons why it is extremely difficult to apply mindfulness to our way of thinking.

1. The first reason that mindfulness is extremely difficult is because we cannot instruct the mind what not to think. If you were asked to close your eyes for 30 seconds and not think about a large elephant on the roof of a house and at the same time you are standing on the lawn wearing a bathing costume in the middle of winter, your mind will insert an image and then remove it e.g., a cut and paste exercise. That is how your mind negates.

2. The second reason that mindfulness is extremely difficult is because we get our sense of self and personal identity through our thoughts. One of the central tenets of Western civilization is Descartes' famous Cogito Ergo Sum: I think, therefore I am. And most of us, of course, are quite fond of our personal identities. It could be argued that most of us are addicted to our own identities.

3. The third reason that mindfulness is extremely difficult is because our minds have a negativity bias. The vast majority of our thoughts are both redundant and negative. This is how our minds are built, primarily as protective devices that attempt to stave off possible future traumas, betrayals and disappointments. As babies we want to eat when we're hungry, sleep when we're tired and play when we feel playful. However, unless you went to a highly progressive school you were soon put on somebody else's schedule. Feeding times are 7:15, noon and 5:30 - not when you're hungry. Sleep times are 8 p.m. to 7 a.m. and nap time -

not when you're tired. In fact, I would daresay that most interactions we have with adults for the first 18 years of our lives are akin to behaviour modification in some way, mostly through receiving positive and negative reinforcement in form of smiles and frowns.

In summary, the three reasons why mindfulness is extremely difficult to most of us is because; We cannot tell the brain what 'not' to think. We get our sense of personal identify through our thoughts, and most of us are rather attached if not addicted to our senses of individual self. As defence mechanisms, our brains have been trained to be biased towards negative thoughts and language to try and fend off possible future harm.

Humans are social creatures. We need social interaction to thrive in life. There is a lot of research to argue that these social interactions can have a devastating effect on our mental health and levels of happiness. When we have healthy social connections it can lead to reducing stress levels, improving our self-image, decreasing our feelings of self-isolation and contributing to our overall feeling of well-being.

While there is research that demonstrates there are positives to social media use, there is also plenty of research that ironically suggests that too much interaction with this technology, designed to help us to connect, can increase feelings of isolation and loneliness and exacerbate mental health issues such as depression and anxiety.

Undoubtedly one of the most powerful benefits of social media is the ability to spread a message or raise awareness for causes to a lot of people in a short amount of time. It gives us the ability to access information and respond to that information much faster than ever before.

On the flip side anyone with a computer or smartphone can share incorrect or misleading information to many people. When used with bad intentions this can be very damaging and create panic and mass hysteria, prompt negative actions towards individuals or groups as well as lead to unhelpful or anti-social behaviour from social media users. It is important that you always do your own research and fact check before reposting information on social media. It does have its uses but I personally feel that most of the time it has a negative impact on others. I have seen and heard (metaphorically speaking being profoundly Deaf) too many *"Facebook wars"* and life is far too short to become embroiled in that sort of thing.

Social media is a great way to link with people and while it is not a substitute for face-to-face interactions, it is a tool to connect with existing friends as well as facilitating new friendships by presenting easy opportunities to find and connect with other like-minded people.

According to social displacement theory, the more time we spend on social media the less time we spend having face to face interactions. These face-to-face interactions release hormones in our brains that help us to feel connected and less lonely, anxious, or depressed. With a decrease in face-to-face interactions there is less of those hormones being released. Some research suggests that people who interacted more through social media rather than face to face were more likely to feel anxious, depressed, lonely and isolated.

CHAPTER TWELVE

POST-TRAUMATIC STRESS DISORDER

"Bad things do happen how I respond to them defines my character and the quality of my life. I can choose to sit in perpetual sadness, immobilized by the gravity of my loss, or I can choose to rise from the pain and treasure the most precious gift I have - life itself."

- Walter Anderson

There are different definitions of post-traumatic stress disorder PTSD. Whilst researching the subject for this book and trying to reflect on how my life has been affected by bad and traumatic experiences, I decided to use the following definitions as they seem to reflect how I felt and feel.

"Post-traumatic stress disorder (PTSD) is a disorder that develops in some people who have experienced a shocking, scary or dangerous event. It is natural to feel afraid during and after a traumatic situation. Fear triggers many split-second changes in the body to help defend against danger or to avoid it."

PTSD was initially attributed to war veterans and was, many years ago, called 'shell shock'. It has been seen that many veterans from both WW1 and WW2 suffered from shell shock. Sadly, some veterans were seen as deserters and were sentenced to death by firing squad. Many years later these people were exonerated.

There are varying symptoms associated with PTSD and the following are some of the signs:

1. A life-threatening event: This includes a perceived-to-be life threatening event. Whether or not it actually is, it's really about the perception of the person who experienced or witnessed the event that it could happen to them again.

2. Internal reminders of the event. These symptoms typically present as nightmares or flashbacks. It's important to realise that these are not simply memories. They are unwanted, intrusive episodes in which a person feels as though they are in the life-threatening situation again - like they're watching a movie or seeing it unfold in front of them. It feels very real to them.

3. Avoidance of external reminders. Those with PTSD often do whatever they can, to not think about their traumatic event, to suppress the feelings associated with it. They might avoid alleys if they were assaulted in one, or they might refuse to drive if they were in a car accident.

4. Altered anxiety state. PTSD can leave people feeling on edge and looking out for danger (hypervigilance). Really what it boils down to is that people feel more anxious.

5. Their startled response is exaggerated. They're jumpy or looking over their shoulder more often. It's a physical reaction to the body's increased anxiety and the need to be aware of possible threats.

6. Changes in mood or thinking. People with PTSD can see the world as a very dangerous place. And because they focus on protecting themselves from it, it's often difficult for them to go out in public. The isolation can lead to depression, or sometimes a person may act in an opposite way when they see no future. In

that case, they may take more risks or engage in risky behaviours.

Adjustment disorder occurs in response to a stressful life event *(or events)*. The emotional or behavioural symptoms a person experiences in response to the stressor are generally more severe or more intense than what would be reasonably expected for the type of event that occurred.

During my earlier years of life my mind was running amok. Anything that happened to me or around me felt like it was worse than it perhaps really was.

I could not reason with myself and tell myself that *'hey, this is not as bad as you think it is.'* Suffering from what I believe is PTSD is debilitating. I was not motivated or had any energy to even do anything if I wanted to. It was as previously described, like living on a hamster wheel or a duck in water. On the surface all looked calm and serene but below the surface, complete panic and mayhem.

Symptoms can include feeling tense, sad or hopeless; withdrawing from other people; acting defiantly or showing impulsive behaviour; or physical manifestations like tremors, palpitations and headaches. The symptoms cause significant distress or problems functioning in important areas of someone's life, for example, at work, school or in social interactions.

Symptoms of adjustment disorders begin within three months of a stressful event and last no longer than six months after the stressor or its consequences have ended.

CHAPTER THIRTEEN

ANGER AND MOOD SWINGS

"I hate my moods; they never ask permission before they change."

- Anonymous

round the time of my friend's death, I was becoming withdrawn and after he had passed away, I blamed the world. I was aggressive and abusive towards people who knew me and towards people I did not know.

I was looking for any opportunity to be argumentative or imposing. This led to a some of altercations verbally. It was something when looking back, that was embarrassing and wrong. I was thoroughly ashamed of my behaviour and manner and have gone some way, over the years, to make amends.

Unfortunately, a few people would not accept my apology or pretended to accept it and over the years have not been approachable, especially when I needed to reach out for support. I do not bear any malice towards them but if I am honest with myself, I am a little disappointed that they haven't accepted that I was unwell at the time.

The stressor may be a single event (such as a romantic breakup) or there may be more than one event with a cumulative effect. Stressors may be recurring or continuous (such as an ongoing painful illness with increasing disability). Stressors may affect a single individual, an entire family or a larger group or community *(for example, in the case of a natural disaster)*.

An estimated 5% to 20% of individuals in outpatient mental health treatment have a principal diagnosis of adjustment disorder. A recent study found that more than 15% of adults with cancer had adjustment disorder. It is typically treated with psychotherapy.

CHAPTER FOURTEEN

FACEBOOK WARS

"There's life without Facebook and the Internet? Really? Send me the link."

- Anonymous

The Urban Dictionary describes Facebook wars as:
'The partaking or observing a heated cyber argument on someone's Facebook wall. Usually it results in one of the parties involved getting their backsides beat at a party by the other people involved.'

Within the concept of Facebook wars is Facebook stalking. This is the phenomenon whereby a Facebook user will regularly visit the site/wall of another user. This becomes so regular that an obsession occurs, which in turn results in a person being a victim of a

Facebook stalker. This is the virtual version of a physical stalker.

The online stalker can remain hidden by fake profiles and once they're detected and removed, they create a new persona and reconnect with their victim. This can be done via your friends contacts where the stalker can be a 'friend' of one of your friends which in turn, makes them a friend of yours, and the stalking then continues under a pseudonym of the original stalker.

The problem as I saw it and still see it, is that people nowadays prefer talking via a social media platform. Before COVID-19 people were constantly asking to be added to my friends list. Around that time I was needing face to face contact and all I was getting was offers to 'chat' online. Meeting people online leads to a virtual life. Life becomes automotive and the enjoyment of meeting someone for a chat and a drink fades away.

From these interactions you risk reading and being told information that is, to coin a phrase, 'fake news'. Donald Trump the American president spoke constantly about fake news. I suspect it was sometimes to his advantage to create a 'story' that hopefully would grow and grow.

Fake news becomes and creates a possible toxic environment. From this, people become suspicious and wary. Paranoia sometimes sets in which goes on to affect and damage our mental health. I found this to be true for myself. I was constantly reading and being told information which I was led to believe was true.

My mental health was deteriorating slowly day by day, month by month. I could not see or recognise this problem back then and it is only with time and being able to be honest and open with myself, I was and am able to reflect on the issues that led to me becoming extremely paranoid about anything I was told. Nowadays, I am still suspicious of what I see and read, what I am told and have heard.

CHAPTER FIFTEEN

FAKE NEWS

"The cure to eliminate fake news is that people stop reading 140-character tweets and start reading 600-page books."

- Piero Scaruffi

Fake news nowadays is seen as referring to political comments etc. Experts say that we should avoid using the words fake news and change it to fake information.

This covers a wider, broader range of topics and seems a more relevant definition. Lots of things you read on social media platforms appear to be true but, in many cases, it is false and has been posted online for a specific reason. It may be there to mislead people and to make them support or follow an idea.

False information is news, stories, or hoaxes to

deliberately misinform or deceive others. False information is not new; however, it has become a hot topic since 2017. Traditionally we got our news from trusted sources, journalists and media outlets that are required to follow strict codes of practice. However, the internet has enabled a whole new way to publish, share and consume information and news with very little regulation or editorial standards.

Many people now get news from social media sites and networks and often it can be difficult to tell whether stories are credible or not. Information overload and a general lack of understanding about how the internet works by people has also contributed to an increase in fake news or hoax stories. Social media sites can play a big part in increasing the reach of these type of stories. (Webwise.ie)

When I was *'active'* on social media platforms, many things I read, I believed. I was convinced that if it was online and others supported or fed into the topic of discussion it must be real. Remember back then I was socially awkward. I was socially unaware and was easily led when it came to receiving information. I was naïve and gullible. Unlike my hearing peers, as a Deaf person with few friends and few Deaf friends, I relied on finding 'friends' online. Going out and meeting people or seeking friends in the community. was practically impossible and thoughts of doing it were quite terrifying. Communication was my biggest fear. I am a BSL user and everyone around me was hearing and did not sign.

Nowadays I try to avoid social media platforms and only have one for my business but I do not have a personal account. This is because I want to be able to protect myself from being exposed to false information, online fighting and discrimination. It is very difficult to assess what it true and what is not.

Whilst researching this topic I found an interesting article produced by Webwise.ie. the article suggested that there were 6 things that would help to identify if information was true or false.

How to spot false information:

1. *Take a closer look;* Check the source of the story, do you recognise the website? Is it a credible/reliable source? If you are unfamiliar with the site, look in the about section or find out more information about the author.

If you are using Facebook is the article something you have been interested in the past or is it a completely new newsfeed? Check the web address and URL.

You can always google the author to see what they have written about in the past. Is the article the sort or work the author is known for?

2. *Look beyond the headline;* Check the entire article, many fake news stories use sensationalist or shocking headlines to grab attention. Often the headlines of fake new stories are in all caps and use exclamation points.

The headlines are usually sensationalised and sound unbelievable. This is one way of drawing the reader in. Further reading of the article may show that the headlines for the article are not in any way, relevant to the article's intent.

3. *Check other sources;* Are other reputable news/media outlets reporting on the story? Are there any sources in the story? If so, check they are reliable or if they even exist!

It is always worth looking at other news outlets. Are they carrying the same story? Bearing in mind that the story might be an exclusive does it look plausible and somewhere else there will be someone who has either printed something similar or not, as the case might be.

Are there any sources within the article that you can search for and see if they're known for being reliable or unreliable etc.

4. *Check the facts;* Stories with false information often contain incorrect dates or altered timelines. It is also a good idea to check when the article was published, is it current or an old news story?

An online search can help to identify specific timelines, dates etc. Look for a chronology, does the article and its content jump back and forth in time or is there a logical order in which, makes the article true. Does the article show irregular dates and dates that 'feel' incorrect or exaggerated?

If this is the case, then there may be a cause to be suspicious of its content and facts?

5. *Check your biases;* Are your own views or beliefs affecting your judgement of a news feature or report?

The article may 'tick' all your boxes in relation to

your own interests and beliefs. The article may be so in line with your own views that your brain decides the article is factually correct. Ask yourself if you were a neutral, would you accept the article as being true? More than likely our bias has a significant effect on what we want to and will believe.

Bias has a strong influence on our decision making and if the article is about something that you feel passionate about be wary and step back, pause for a moment and ask yourself, is it me or is the article true?

6. *Is it a joke?* Satirical sites are popular online and sometimes it is not always clear whether a story is just a joke or parody… Check the website, is it known for satire or creating funny stories?

Satire is prevalent in articles and the author/s may have a satirical stance when presenting their news articles. Check the author, are they known for being satirical and humorous? Is the source a *'tongue in cheek'* style of reporter? Is the story compared with other news outlets versions carrying a hint of sarcasm or wit? Is this their style of reporting? The article could be factual but has been *'tweaked'* to entertain their target audience and readership?

I remember when I was in my teenage years, there were a lot of social media attacks within the Deaf community itself, these attacks were encouraging negative feelings within the Deaf community. I know all communities have their problems, but at the time I remember feeling shocked that such a small close knit community would do this. This happened on various social media platforms. The fact that it was a Deaf-on-Deaf attack as such, made me wonder what it was that made a minority group accept *'infighting'* as the *'norm'*.

If it was hearing people attacking the views and trying to cause a falling out with Deaf people, I could possibly understand that. Historically the Deaf community have had to fight tooth and nail for recognition within society.

Educationalists who advised parents of Deaf children, which route to take educationally, which communication method to adopt within and outside the family home, and what would be best for the *'child'* were all hearing. There was no understanding of *'Deaf Culture'* or *'Deafhood'*.

All the *'experts'* were from the hearing community. No one thought to investigate or ask members of the

Deaf community for their viewpoint. These were Deaf people with years and years of experience, who could advise parents better than their hearing peers.

The experiences I had with social media, fake news and cyber bullying were horrendous. I recognise how extreme that sounds, but at the time it felt horrendous and unbearable, and sometimes unfortunately even today this still happens - in all communities. I just wonder why people in all communities, especially those smaller communities who need each other's support more, cannot just get along with each other. When I was younger, I had a particularly horrible experience, I was bullied through social media. At the time I was playing for a Deaf football club, all of the players, including myself, had a variety of skills. However at the time, I had a real passion and found myself very skilful. Like all young children at the time who loved football, I aspired to be as good as David Beckham or Cristiano Ronaldo - I started to copy their style and focused my skills on both of their football skills, especially freekicks. I was very keen on the importance of teamwork and just assumed everyone else had that same viewpoint. Sadly, that wasn't the case, two boys from the club set up a fake profile and started bullying me online through this account - this continued for around 5 months and it was constant. It made me feel wretched and made me feel so unwell, physically and mentally. I still don't know why they both decided to do what they did, I feel it could have been out of jealousy due to my football skills, however regardless of the skill level of us all, we all still should have worked together to our strengths, not bully others because of the different skills that they may have. After a long 5 months of bullying I decided to report it to Facebook.

Unfortunately, back then and even nowadays, Facebook did nothing about it and allowed it to carry on, insofar as their lack of interest and their intention, to not follow up my complaint or remove their profiles, this gave the 2 guys a *free* licence and permission to carry on hurting me. That is when, I decided to close my personal Facebook account forever. Since then I have never used Facebook on a personal basis and I will never return to use it again.

CHAPTER SIXTEEN

DEAF CULTURE

"The problem is not that the deaf can't hear. The problem is that the hearing won't listen."

- Rev. Jesse Jackson 1988

eaf culture has many different meanings. The Deaf Culture Centre in Toronto, Ontario Canada published an interesting article on Deaf culture. They looked at what constitutes Deaf culture. They posed three questions:

1. Where do we find Deaf culture?
2. Who decides that this is a culture?
3. What constitutes Deaf culture?

They concluded that,

'Deaf Culture is the heart of the Deaf community everywhere in the world. Language and culture are inseparable. They are

intertwined and passed down through generations of Deaf people.'

In the UK the Deaf community use various ways of communicating with each other and people outside of their community.

There are various styles of communication and one of those is British Sign Language (BSL). This is used by a large majority of Deaf people and one of the more favoured ways to communicate with each other. BSL has its own grammar and vocabulary. It is not a sign for word equivalent to English. BSL is a rich and visual language. It has a unique structure and word *(sign)* order. It is the language of many grassroot Deaf people.

The Deaf community is not based on geographic proximity like Chinatown or the Italian District for example. The Deaf community is comprised of culturally Deaf people who appreciate their heritage, history, literature and culture. Many people in the Deaf community use a sign language *e.g., BSL, Signed Supported English (SSE), Signed Exact English (SEE).*

The Deaf community is also comprised of other people who use the language and have an attitude that makes them an accepted part of the community though they may not be in the core of the community. It exists because of the need to get together, the need to relax and socialise while being together.

Deaf culture exists because Deaf people who are educated at residential Deaf schools develop their own Deaf network once they graduate, to keep in touch with everyone. Most of them go on to take positions in the Deaf community, organize Deaf sports, community events, etc. and become the core of the Deaf community. They ensure that their language and heritage are passed to other peers and to the next generation. They also form links with parents and siblings of Deaf children to strengthen and enlarge the community circle for Deaf children.

In the UK we have the British Deaf Association (BDA) who are one of the main organisations that work with and promote the Deaf community.

The National Deaf Children's Society (NDCS), work with families of Deaf children and campaign for those individuals and support them throughout their childhood and support them through their education until adulthood.

Both organisations, alongside others, aim to

promote both the language and culture of the Deaf community. They provide advocacy support as and when required and support people around issues of mental health.

Both organisations have representation on a political level and are used as advisors when government propose new policies.

According to the Deaf Culture Centre (DCC) they argue that:

'Language and culture are interrelated. Sign language (1) is central to any Deaf person, child or adult for their intellectual, social, linguistic and emotional growth but to truly internalize the language, they must have the culture that is embedded in the language. Every linguistic and cultural group has its own way of seeing and expressing how they see and interpret the world and interact in it.' (Deaf Culture Centre, Toronto, Ontario, Canada)

Culture consists of language, values, traditions, norms and identity (Padden, 1980).

Unfortunately due to the lack of intervention, support and bullying that resulted in my experience when I was younger, my view of parts of the Deaf community is different to what others experienced. My experience through my childhood and the support from organisations like NDCS was non-existent. I was nearly 10 years old before somebody recognised that I wasn't in the correct school, that I needed access to BSL and taught in BSL, not English. The NDCS is a brilliant organisation who support many families and Deaf children, however somehow I slipped through the net and received no help from them. I feel if I received help and was directed to them, my whole upbringing and sense of identity and acceptance would have been so much clearer.

This was the organisation that boasted that their role was to support Deaf children through the educational system. They state that they support families who have Deaf children and are there to advise parents whenever they need help or support. My mother never received any support at all, she struggled along on her own. The Deaf organisations and their representatives were not kicking down our front door. If anything, they were completely invisible and absent when we were looking for advice, help and support.

Reading this, to some, it may seem I am still bitter and if I am honest, I am still bitter and I feel robbed of a service that should have been received to support my development, sense of inclusivity and education. When my mother asked for help she didn't receive it, for what reason we still do not know. It felt and still does feel disappointing, that these organisations who promote to support families with Deaf children so much didn't or couldn't, support us. I would like to hope that access to this service would have been improved over time and they are able to benefit all those who require help.

As I got older and entered my college years and up to and beyond the age of 21 I hoped that organisations like the BDA and others would be there for me. Unfortunately, it was a struggle for my mother and I to access sufficient help around that time. This was when I lost my close friend and really needed support. All the medical profession wanted to do is provide a pharmaceutical approach to treat my issues. I was and still am suspicious around taking tablets and medication. I was paranoid about becoming drug dependant and that was the last thing I wanted to be.

CHAPTER SEVENTEEN

TIME TO REFLECT

"Reflection is one of the most underused yet powerful tools for success."

- Richard Carlson

Looking back at my experiences I had with some members of the Deaf community, bearing in mind my delayed experiences with the community and lack of communication skills, I decided to distance myself from the Deaf community. This was not a decision I took lightly and it still makes me sad to this day that I don't have a lot of Deaf friends because of my journey, how the lack of inclusion from a young age made me feel and the cyber bullying I suffered from a few Deaf 'friends'. I really feel that things could have been very different if I was supported from a young age by professionals to enable me to communicate with other members of the community. Still to this day due to my experiences, I am always wary of meeting new people due to the potential backstabbing from both hearing and Deaf communities - it's always a worry of mine.

My decision to withdraw from the community I thought was there to support me was mine alone. I have not been influenced or persuaded by others. It has been a difficult choice and I know I have been criticised by others. The backstabbing and I am sorry to use such strong words, but it is exactly how I feel, has been dreadful and caused me a lot of issues when I was younger. It was so bad that it had a detrimental effect on my mental health. People were so cruel towards me for reasons I am unaware of to this day, that I became suicidal. At that time, I really did not want to live any longer. I had constant thoughts of dying and trying to work out which was the easiest guaranteed way of killing myself. This was because people who perhaps didn't even know me, thought it was okay to be abusive. These people never for one moment *(I suspect)* realised what effect their cruel words and actions would have on me or others. To use words and cruel comments that push someone over the edge is pretty much disgraceful and shame on those people. I have no qualms about being blunt and saying these words. These people are bullies, they are parasitical and they are the worst of the worst. Fuck social media!

CHAPTER EIGHTEEN

MOVING ON

"The truth is, unless you let go, unless you forgive yourself, unless you forgive the situation, unless you realize that the situation is over, you cannot move forward."

\- Steve Maraboli

After many years of being bullied and feelings of despair. I decided it was time to move on. I had several choices of which one was a pharmaceutical approach. I was encouraged to go and see my GP and explain how I was feeling. At the appointment, I felt the GP wasn't listening to what I was telling them because they kept repeating that medication would be needed to be taken on a regular basis.

This was a very paranoid Deaf man sat in front of him. He was being told that you must take your medication as this will help you to relax and start to feel better. I was not going to listen to them, especially in the state that I was at that time. Medication on a regular basis sent my paranoia into overdrive. I had no desire to take the medication and then become dependent on tablets for who knew how long? I had heard and seen many people who took the advice of their GP's and became so dependent on their medication that they could not function without it. I did not want to be like them. I could imagine that if I became dependent on the medication my GP was suggesting, I would be like a robot, barely functioning for myself.

After leaving the GP I went home and with my mother being unaware and who was extremely concerned about my appearance both physically and mentally, I flushed the tablets down the toilet.

Deciding to refuse medication made me feel liberated, and for the first time in my life I started to feel a little better. I realised it was now entirely up to me, what I should do next…

I started off by setting up a regular fitness regime. I strongly believed a healthy body leads to a healthy mind. Originally, this is a Latin saying - Mens sana in corpore sano - which translates to *"a healthy body can sustain a healthy mind".* We often hear this phrase as friendly advice or as the slogan of our favourite lifestyle brands. However, this phrase holds a powerful meaning and the key to a better and, in some cases, longer life. Developing a healthy body and a healthy mind through a stronger connection between the two, can have a significant effect on your well-being.

My fitness regime started with doing weight training at a local gym which unfortunately closed so I purchased a set of weights and worked from home. I trained every day and incorporated press ups and sit ups into my routine. After a period I needed something that would invigorate me and make me feel good. I started running, building up my distance's week by week. Today I can run about 10-12 miles on each session. My aim eventually I guess, will be to run a half marathon. The running and pounding the streets where I live help me to clear my mind completely. It is like a mental detox.

I was researching this chapter and came across a good quote which for me, sums up the belief of a healthy body and mind.

"Peace of mind is the basis of a healthy body and a healthy mind; so peace of mind, a calm mind, is very, very important." (Dalai Lama)

What is being said here is, if you want a healthy body and mind you must be able to be at peace with yourself and others. You must maintain a calm mind, removing all negative thoughts and be positive instead. If you possess these skills and abilities, treat them with respect and do not be *'matter of fact'* in your everyday life.

I aim each day to be as positive as I can possibly be. If I am having a stressful day, or, I am unable to think positively, I will go for a punishing run. This will *'clean'* my mind and hopefully *'wash'* away any negative thoughts or feelings I am having.

CHAPTER NINETEEN

CHANGING FROM THE NEGATIVE TO THE POSITIVE

"It takes but one positive thought when given a chance to survive and thrive to overpower an entire army of negative thoughts."

- Robert H. Schuller

I realised quite quickly that negativity limits your potential to becoming something great and to enable yourself to have and experience a fulfilling, and purposeful life. I also noticed it had a palpable effect on my health.

While researching this book, I discovered from various sources, that people like myself who have cultivated negative energy, experience more stress, they will feel unwell more than usual. In my experience this has led to less opportunities in my life, especially when I was younger. I realised that learning how to get rid of negative energy had a significant effect on my mental health.

When we decide to become positive and follow that up with action we also begin to encounter situations and people that are also positive. In other words, if you *'hang out'* with positive people you are able to disengage from negative types and life becomes more rewarding. All the negativity energy gets kicked into touch because of your positive experiences and becomes like a snowball effect, which means it grows and grows and is better for your mental health and well-being.

I accept that negative and positive energy will always exist. The key to becoming positive is to reduce the amount of negativity in your life. The way to do this, is to fill your life with more positivity.

During my short lifetime it is easy when life is all about us, we believe quite easily, that we deserve what we have. We feel that we are entitled to be put at the centre of the universe as such. We then have unrealistic expectations and expect that others should cater for our needs and our wants.

This vanity is a guaranteed way to set yourself up for an unfulfilled life of negative thoughts and feelings.

If you really want to learn how to get rid of negative energy step back, look at your life so far and decide *'roll up your sleeves'* and work hard to change.

Living this type of lifestyle and belief of *'entitlement'* is an *'energy sucker'*. We tend to search for what we can get out of any given situation. I realised that I did not appreciate the nuances within my lifestyle and the constant state of lacking something. To live life like this results in it being difficult to live a positive one.

When we spend time being grateful and appreciate what is going on in our lives, from the small struggles that make us feel better, to the *'car'* that gets us from A to B every day, we shift our attitude from one of lack and frustration to one of appreciation. This appreciation and change of attitude gets noticed by others and from this a more positive, harmonious existence begins to form and improves our relationships with others. We begin to receive more of that which we are grateful for because we have 'opened' ourselves up to the notion of receiving rather than taking. This will ensure your life becomes more fulfilling and more positive.

I decided to look for new relationships that were not toxic or from the past. It was time to move on. I knew that this would result in being accused of being too good for others. I would and was accused of being arrogant and appearing elitist.

All I was trying to do was to make a fresh start. For years I had been on a negative, downward spiral, and now it was time to drag myself up by my laces and focus on a better lifestyle. It was not and is still not easy. It has been the most difficult thing I have done in my life. I had suffered abuse and bullying at school. I had been physically assaulted and abused in so many ways as a young adult in the employment arena.

My new employment is with a small company. They have been fantastic for my mental health even though the world has been embroiled in Covid and its variants. I have never felt more supported in my life and it feels like a breath of fresh air and a new chapter in my life.

I have learnt so many things over the last few years and have also faced adversity of many kinds. My life is a busy one and I have a full schedule. I guess my work can feel from time to time, task-oriented and routine driven. Do not get me wrong, I love my job and love working for the company I am working for.

Being human can feel more like being a robot. However, I recognise having this work-driven serious attitude often results in negative energy and performance-orientated thinking.

When I decided to go down the path of positivity, I realised the best way to do that was to not take life too seriously and not worry too much about what I was doing. My view is you only live life once so why not be happy and laugh rather than be doom and gloom all of the time. They say laughter is a good tonic and good for your well-being, I fully endorse that and ensure that I am feeling happy every day. Laughter helps to remind me that being positive means taking life less seriously.

In the past I was very sensitive to sarcasm and had trouble laughing at jokes. I am not sure if it was because of my mental health at the time or something different? I think it was because my life was entirely connected to work and I had no opportunities to socialise on a non-work basis. I knew that if I could laugh at myself and laugh at any mistakes I had made then my life would become more of an experiment in finding out what made me happy and enabling me to find happiness which in turn, made finding positivity a lot easier.

Negativity goes hand in hand with selfishness. If I continued to live just for myself it would lead to having no higher purpose in life. If the whole point of this world is only to take care of yourself and no one else, my road to long-term fulfilment and purpose was going to be a long one. I knew that to be able get rid of negative energy I had to look outside of myself and begin to help others. I care and look after my mother every day and I am always there for her.

I decided to do the sponsored walk as a way of giving something back rather than just taking. This was a rewarding experience for me and made me feel very positive about life. A few years back I would not have paused for a second to think about doing these things.

We become most like the people we surround ourselves with. If your friends or work group are full of negative-energy suckers. These people suck the positivity out of life like leeches sucking on blood. In my previous employments, I was surrounded by these people and real-life drama queens.

What this did for me was to make me like them. Any positivity inside of me was sucked from me and replaced with toxicity, animosity, jealousy and hatred for others who achieved more than me.

In this situation, it is very difficult to become more positive when the people around me were not supportive or constantly failed to demonstrate positive behaviour.

As I became more positive, I found that my former friends and work colleagues had a choice to either appreciate the new me or become resistant to my positive changes. Alas the majority chose the latter. I did not criticise their decision making as I discovered that it was the norm and a natural response from human beings.

Change is extremely scary. For me, cutting out the negative people was a huge step in becoming more positive. I found that positive people reflected and bounced their perspectives on to me and others. Positivity, for me, was a step-by-step process especially because I was doing it on my own, a group of positive friends makes it feel like an escalator. What I mean is that life was onwards and upwards. If I was on a down escalator I was not too worried because I knew it would lead me to another path, one where I could look to move forward and upwards in my life choices and style.

I did not realise at the time that negative energy can be overwhelming and challenging to navigate. Negativity is usually accompanied by a *'freak-out'* response, especially when linked to relationships of any kind, people and worrying about what the future could hold for me. This I found, was extremely debilitating to me and my path to positivity. This had further negative, more worrying, more stress and more freak-out moments. The only way to resolve this was to turn all the negativity into positivity. Discarding negative thoughts to then convert them to more positive thinking. When I was in one of those situations and was feeling bad I would walk away and take a break. With my eyes closed, I would take a few deep breaths. Once I was calm again I would sit and think about how to approach the problem. I would try and come up with 4-5 alternatives to enable me to solve the problem. Taking myself out of the emotionally charged negativity by moving into an action-orientated positive, helped me to solve more problems rationally and live a more positive lifestyle.

If I was facing a problem that could not be solved in a matter of minutes taking a break still benefitted me. I would go out for a walk or a run or do a short workout. I found it helped me to clear my head, which in turn, enabled me to think more clearly. This helped me to think more clearly and help to resolve the problem I was having.

CHAPTER TWENTY

THE PATH OF NEGATIVITY

"If you ever walk down a path surrounding by negative energy.
Look for the fork in the bath then cross over to the positive
side."

\- Victoria Addino

To become a more positive person you need to first identify what negativity is and what a negative person 'looks' like. There are many indicators and some of the more common ones, I believe are, constant worrying, complaining about everything and anything, a lack of confidence, doom and gloom attitude and anxiety. These indicators can be soul destroying. These indicators or traits are common among negative people. As we are all aware, there are always good and bad times. This is a recognised phenomenon and is accepted as the norm. I try to think, *'this will pass, and tomorrow is another day'*.

The difficult task is to recognise that negative person. Who is this person, who is out to ruin our lives and make our lives a misery? What are the warning signs and indicators we are looking for?

The negative person in the crowd will be the one that is always worrying. They are the people who thrive on doom and gloom. It feeds them like an addict needing alcohol etc. They are always anticipating the worst, even when things appear to be going okay for them. The negative person always appears pessimistic. They can never see the brighter side of life. Small situations for these people are thought of as catastrophic when they are trivial. Whether it is being stuck in traffic or experiencing a bad day they think the worst.

No matter what others try to do to encourage the person, they can never put a smile on the negative persons face. The negative person rarely sees a positive, happy outcome or result. They always imagine that everything will go wrong.

Negative people with persistent negative views always complain a lot. Since they complain regularly it results in making people feel frustrated and leaves a feeling of unpleasantness. They believe that the whole world is against them. They will constantly complain about anything and even complain about something that is seen to be trivial.

Negative people remain within their comfort zone. They are constantly weary of the possibility of more fear, discomfort, challenges or failures. Therefore, the negative person can never try out new things or new ventures and are generally living on a *'hamster wheel'* of being dull and boring. This situation only encourages the negative person to not try and change for the best.

Lack of success could be due to many factors, but the main cause is negativity. Negative people have a belief that they are not as smart as others, not athletic enough, or good enough, in general. The real problem is threat to their success. This is because their emotional intelligence is debilitated by their often critical and negative attitude. As far as they are concerned, their future does not excite them. They do not see any possibility of digging themselves out of a rut. They are never open to the idea of changing their beliefs and attitude, this is because they do not look beyond the present, their misery or perceived misery. Their life could be best described as being stuck in an endless dark tunnel with no chink of light at the end of it. They live in perpetuity. Their lives exist for the present and there are no plans or aspirations for the future.

During my *'darker years'* I was living in perpetuity and my life never extended from the present. I had no plans at all for the future and this I believe was why I went to the brink of suicide. I could not see ahead, I could not even think of tomorrow, let alone long-term.

I was miserable, feeling morose and wretched. My life was going nowhere, I was not travelling through a tunnel of darkness, it was a journey spiralling downwards into hell. I know it sounds dramatic but, that is exactly how I felt. There were no plans no aspirations, no ambitions or aims and targets. My life was mind numbingly boring. I was living a *'groundhog'* existence. It was an effort to get out of bed in the morning, my self-motivation was non-existent. From the outside I must have appeared antisocial, rude, arrogant and presenting as a could not care attitude. Continuing in a negative way was draining and I felt as though my very existence was slowly being sucked dry. I felt physically and emotionally drained and void of any feelings. The more I engaged with people of a similar lifestyle the worse I felt and I needed to set myself free of them and focus my energies elsewhere.

After I walked away from the edge of the cliff I had been standing on and contemplating to take one more step into the void, I decided I had to sort myself out and vow to never go back to the way I had been living. The aim was to change my lifestyle 180 degrees. With hard work, determination and strength I discovered that nothing is impossible.

Negative thinking was constant and too often it was harmful to my body, mind, and soul.

Each time I had a negative thought I would try and redirect it to a positive channel. I learnt that I had to find the positive within the negativity that was present. It was going to be difficult but would become easier with regular practice.

In the long run I discovered I was more relaxed and began to enjoy life a whole lot more than I had in the past. It was a revelation and at times overwhelming, which in turn had a deep impact on my emotional wellbeing, which had to be good for me long term. When I started to look forward to something I noticed that my mind was remaining proactive. I began to feel fully functional. So I decided to plan my day with things that gave me real happiness, this in turn, aided my quest to think positively.

Life is too short to only do what you are focused to do. This could return to being stuck in a rut which was not conducive for me. I decided that I had to step outside my comfort zone. This was why taking part in Karate and MMA helped me to regain my focus and was certainly way beyond what I was used to.

In my opinion, belief is all that mattered. As a person you can do anything you put your mind to. If you start to think that you can't change your thinking, then it is likely that you won't. However, with starting out with a positive mindset, just about anything is possible. I had to believe that good things would happen and things I had planned would come to fruition.

CHAPTER TWENTY-ONE

THE PATH TO RECOVERY

"Recovery is something that you have to work on every single day, and it's something that doesn't get a day off."

- Demi Lovato

Nothing is ever permanent, that's one fact that nobody can chip away at. I needed time to digest that fact, knowing that if I did, then it would be a lot easier to start thinking and acting positively. Nothing was set in stone, and I worked extremely hard on changing the things that I was unhappy with. It wasn't just relationships and what I mean by that, is the company I was involved with, it also involved my health and professional life too. I had worked for several employers who had been both physically and emotionally abusive towards me.

Whilst working with one company I had been physically assaulted as I have explained earlier in this book. My Deafness was targeted and mimicked. People I was supposed to be working alongside, were working against me. I needed to do something straightaway or I would have been dragged further down and it would have made me even more unwell. I was already extremely depressed. I was feeling paranoid as I felt everyone was out to *'get me'*. Looking back, I now know, that this was my responsibility as I was the only person who understood me properly.

Others around me thought they knew me but my exterior persona was a fake one. I had been faking it for many years and needed to step up and show people who I really was. I was Shaun Fitzgerald, the Deaf guy with a rebuilt mind.

CHAPTER TWENTY-TWO

FROM OUT OF THE DARKNESS AND INTO THE LIGHT

"Sometimes you have to go through darkness to get to get to the light."

- Anonymous

From out of the darkness, I knew there would be light. I knew that no matter how hard I would try, I was going to still have some negativity in my life. Life is a mixture of ups and downs, highs and lows, laughter and tears, happiness, and sadness. We all have our own struggles and most of us come out unscathed on the other side.

I had many scars, some visible and some not so visible. We all carry scars that we tend to bury deep within ourselves but, sometimes when they are buried so deep we can have a toxic reaction to varying situations and life in general. The most important thing to do is to try and look for the good in every situation. Doing this may result in a pleasant surprise for you and others.

Life throws various kinds of obstacles in our path. Sometimes we have periods of time when all is well and at other times it can seem as if every bad omen is heading our way, as we bounce from one emotionally draining crisis to another. What surprises me is that some people manage to keep going irrespective of what's happening around them. Initially, I found this practicably impossible, especially when I was starting my journey towards positivity. I asked myself, if the circumstances for each person are the same, why do some cope really well yet others are sucked under? I realised quite soon that developing a positive lifestyle has more to do with how you choose to perceive situations than about the actual situations themselves. No one can feel positive all the time and it is argued whether that would be a good thing anyway. If everything in life was positive how would you as a person be motivated to work harder. Would we become complacent? I think complacency would be your biggest nemesis. Life would become mundane and commonplace. Remember, our appreciation of the things we have, tends to be greater when we have had to strive to get or keep it.

Current research and the views of those who are in the know, suggests a healthy and positive lifestyle has nothing to do with looks, money or status, although it could make life easier to have these. Anyone can develop a positive lifestyle if you ensure it becomes a habit.

One of the first things I learnt when starting out on my path to living positively was to *'let go'*. I needed to work out how much time I was going to waste wishing things or people were 'different'. It was useless thinking *'if only this'*, *'if only that'*, what happens cannot be undone so why compound the issue with throwing good after bad?

We all preferred things to be different but what is in the past should remain in the past. It would be a waste of time and excessive frustration trying to change things. If you go over the same ground again and again in your head means you are fighting reality. This type of *'groundhog'* thinking exhausts and stops you from benefitting from a positive way of being and having a positivity approach to life.

The way to challenge your thinking is to let go by taking a deep breath and telling yourself *'Okay'*, I would have liked things to be different but if I keep on thinking this way, I will make things worse rather than better.

CHAPTER TWENTY-THREE

RECOGNISING THE REAL ME

"Here's to the people who know the real me but still stick around."

\- Unknown

As a person I needed to stop putting myself down. When I put myself down it decreased my ability to live in a positive way. It was okay being modest but I needed to make sure I was not being downright passive.

Passive people generally, are not happy positive people. If I was going to stop putting myself down, I needed to learn to look people in the eye, smile, hold myself upright and say *'thank you'* when someone was telling me that things were fine.

I had to learn to stop being negative by saying things like *I'm useless, I can't, or it is always me that gets it wrong*'. I needed to change tack and say, *I found that hard, or I guess it will take a bit more practice*'. I found that it was hard for me to do, but statements such as these meant that I was in control and not becoming the victim e.g., *"woe is me"*.

Thoughts are something we constantly have, and they are funny things that can play tricks with our minds. They make us act in ways that can be detrimental to us and others. Imagine walking down the street and you see someone you recognise on the other side of the street; you smile and wave to them but they do not respond. What would you immediately think? 'Oh they didn't see me, or what have I done wrong?' You have choice, you can tell yourself something negative and immediately feel crap, or you can change the way you think, into something that makes you feel better about yourself, the other person and the world.

To be honest, when you think about it, why would you choose to go down the path of thinking the worst, what would be the sense in doing that? When we make mistakes we shouldn't beat ourselves up because it proves that we are only human. However, many people including myself, end up feeling ashamed, guilty, depressed and anxious.

Back when I was younger I can honestly say that I ticked all the boxes when it came to making mistakes. When I had these feelings, instead of accepting them I realised they were based on what I thought of myself and the situation I tended to find myself in. When I found myself thinking thoughts like *'what will people think?'* I would ask myself what evidence I have that people will think anything at all, let alone anything negative. How would I know that people think in a certain way?

Once I started looking for the evidence to support my self-defeating thinking, I was surprised and amazed how hard it was to find or even find it at all.

No one is going to make anything happen for you so make it happen for yourself. There was never a queue of people or even a single person lining up to do it for me. Even when someone had treated me badly and there were enough of them to do so, you can turn things around.

If I had been unlucky myself I knew it was up to me to sort it out, not someone else. If I personalised a bad situation it made me believe that I was being singled out for bad treatment and I was more unlikely to have success or even a chance of any success. It was a tough, hard lesson to learn but I realised that I was just another statistic. When organisations downsize, make redundancies, good people lose their jobs through no fault of their own.

Sometimes parents are not up to the job of raising children themselves and make mistakes. You cannot help what happened as that child, but you could learn to take responsibility as an adult.

You can shape your future but only if you learn to be brave and take risks. Positive people take risks even if they are scared. (Gladeana 2017)

As a human being I did not want to get hurt and therefore, built a wall that surrounded me metaphorically speaking. I started to believe that people were untrustworthy, and I was determined to keep those people out at all costs. I was blatantly obvious by making sure I was hard to talk to and to get to know. Sometimes I would be very subtle about it by appearing open but ensured that I avoided any meaningful emotional contact. I withdrew from society as such and almost became reclusive. I acknowledged that if I kept people out then I wouldn't get hurt. However, I hurt myself because acting like this resulted in me not being able to live positively, I realised that I had to include people in my life.

Eventually it became clear to me that life is full of people and those who make good relationships are those likely to be happy and get more of what they want from life.

The important thing to remember was that you did not have to be a pushover but make sure you gave people a chance. How many times have you meant to do something and then never got round to doing it, whatever it was? There were many occasions when this happened to me. Laziness drains your confidence and your potential for a positive life. We all need to be lazy and slovenly sometimes but we don't really mean to be. We tend to say we will do that later or tomorrow etc. For many of us tomorrow never comes and putting things off is one more excuse to avoid making the most of life and of your chances in life.

CHAPTER TWENTY-FOUR

SINK OR SWIM

"No matter what grief or loss takes place, most of life flows on all around us, as though nothing's changed. At some point in our sorrow, we each make a choice to sink or swim. There's no alternative."

- Tammara Webber

Motivation is an individual thing, not a shared one, and you, not others, need to find a method that works best for yourself.

Being positive all the while I think, is impossible. The skill is in managing the negativity effectively. If it is not dealt with sufficiently, it will grow and grow until it becomes the dominant thing in your everyday life.

We will always experience negative thoughts and feelings because we are human beings, and it is a natural occurrence. We are not automatons or live a *'robotic'* life, even if our day sometimes feel like that.

Life is always evolving and changes in an instance and we need to be ready to embrace these changes. If we are caught on the *'back foot'* metaphorically speaking, we can fall back into old habits and let negative events suck us dry. It is all about our mindset. My mindset was always *'logged'* into negative feelings, thoughts, ideas and decisions. The concept of positivity was non-existent and was never on my *'radar'*.

I have thought many times about how I perceive negativity as a visual representation, especially being Deaf. As a Deaf person, visual representation helps me to perceive and understand concepts easier. Hearing people rely on listening and looking at the same time to gain information and knowledge. My visual representation of a negative lifestyle is akin to tidal flow. When the tide at a seaside goes out we are left with a vast emptiness and for a period we have a void. As we wait patiently, the tide finally turns and the sea comes back to the land. The sea ebbs and flows and similarly our life and my life has done the same.

Every now and then we have a tidal phenomenon called a Tsunami. This is where the sea is sucked completely away from civilisation and after a period it returns with an anger that is uncontrollable and rushes back to land and has built such a momentum that it extends further than normal and destroys everything in its path. That pretty much sums up my experiences and I suspect, others also.

The Tsunami is overwhelming and so is a life of constant negativity, where everything you see and breathe is negative and damaging to your health. It takes society a long time to recover from the damage the Tsunami has caused.

With having mental health issues, it takes longer. I personally don't believe there is a quick fix. Trying to become positive and live a positive lifestyle and have a positive outlook on life is not a quick fix either. I personally, have been trying for the last 10 years and still have moments of darkness. I still experience the ebb and flow of negativity and sometimes I get close to my *'Tsunami'* moment.

CHAPTER TWENTY-FIVE

PAUSE FOR THOUGHT

"I've always thought you should be able to freeze time. This way you could hit the pause button at a really good point in your life so that nothing changes."

- Jennifer Niven

I do not think in this book I can create a checklist of *'how to move from a negative state to a positive state'*. All I can do is tell you what I have tried to do.

My experiences may seem like yours, but I guess we are all different otherwise society would be tiresome if we were all the same.

So, how do you move form a negative state to a positive state? Firstly, you must want to change. This is applicable to lots of things in life. The alcoholic or heavy drinker who wants to reduce or stop drinking. We have dry January and people try to not drink for a month, but this is just a short-term fix. If we had a *'don't be negative November'*, would it help to change our lifestyle, I don't think it would. To change something you must first, acknowledge that you have a problem. Once you recognise this then you can move forward and progress.

Accepting that you are negative is a double whammy I guess, because I suspect as I did, that you believe you are the same as everyone else. Listening to someone telling you the truth about your manner is never going to be welcomed or accepted as your mindset perceives the world is against you and out to get you and along with mental health issues, you build a defensive barrier that envelops and surrounds you. The more you are reminded of the way you are the higher you build your wall.

With all tall structures, if your foundations are not solid or secure you run the risk of the wall collapsing inwardly and on top of you and burying you alive. Getting to the stage where you finally see that you need to change is difficult and is against everything you believe in. You have spent a long time creating this world you are living in. you have gorged yourself on negativity. You have consumed everything that is bad for you via social media platforms etc. The information you are sourcing is there to suck people in and the more you are sucked in the more successful is the aim of the information givers.

We live in a world of fake news. Fake news encourages discussion and the more people talk about it the more we sign up to it. For me, it was all about people being cruel and enjoying the fact that people like me were being slowly sucked dry. I am not sure what their intentions were. Was it to see how effective and damaging they can be or, was it that they did not have any understanding how their comments, views and opinions affected me and others?

Every day, no matter how hard I tried to avoid this toxicity, I was constantly drawn back to see if they had left me alone. Each and every time I was drawn back I became embroiled in their conversations, which in turn made me depressed, angry, upset and sad. I decided that I needed to draw a line in the sand and promise myself not to go back and forth between everyday life and social media platforms. I deleted my personal Facebook account and my other online accounts. I stopped watching the news and only looked at it on the odd occasion to find out what was happening in the outside world.

Once I had left my online platforms behind me, I felt completely liberated but at the same time I felt scared being *'on my own'* per se. My only contact with the outside world was via social media as I didn't really have *'real'* friends.

Sadly due to the difficulties that I have faced, this has resulted in me not being confident enough to just walk out and strike up a conversation with others. I had withdrawn from mixing with the Deaf community at local Deaf clubs and gatherings. Some of the people from these communities were the instigators of my negativity and rather than isolate myself from specific people, I decided to withdraw completely. Looking back, I think this was an overreaction but at the time I was feeling so overwhelmed that I thought the best way of starting off, was to have a clean slate from where to start. Having a clean slate made things slightly easier as it enabled me to not worry about picking and choosing who to speak to and who not to. Even to this present day, I have not fully returned to Deaf events or gatherings, due to my experiences that have scarred me mentally. I have a select few people from the Deaf community that I am in touch with who have supported my journey and support my achievements, and to them I am very grateful for their friendship. I have always wondered what would happen if I returned fully to the Deaf community again, but I do still have a fear that the same bullying would return from some members. I have worked extremely hard over the last ten years to change my life around and become *'positive Shaun'*. I am generally happier as a person and I am successful in my working part of life. I have my own business that I run at the weekend and evenings, whilst concentrating on my paid employment during the week as a web developer.

Going back to the time when I became disengaged from others, I felt very lonely, and I was starting to think that changing my lifestyle wasn't good for me. My mental health wasn't great either and I started to challenge my actions. I began to believe that perhaps being negative and having that lifestyle was better for me in the long run. It took a lot of willpower to convince myself to stick with the 'plan' and forge onwards and upwards.

CHAPTER TWENTY-SIX

FAMILY TIES AND LIFE BEYOND

"Families are like branches on a tree. We grow in different directions, yet our roots remain as one."

- Unknown

I remember back in 2014 I was attending a Search Engine Optimisation (SEO) course. This is a process that is used to optimise a websites technical configuration, content relevance and link popularity, so it's pages can become easily findable, makes more relevant and popular towards user search queries and consequently, search engines rank them better.

Two weeks prior to the course, my grandmother who I was extremely close to, had been admitted to hospital as she was very poorly. I didn't want to go on the course which I had paid for myself as I wanted to be with her. My mother and grandmother told me to go on the course as it would be beneficial to me when looking for employment.

Reluctantly, I decided to listen to them and go to London. The course went well and upon my return home, I asked my mum how Grandma was, and she told me she had died that same day. I was distraught and was screaming. I wish I had never gone to London as if I had stayed at home, I would have been with her when she passed away.

I was overwhelmed with emotion and could not stop crying. It felt as though part of my heart had been ripped out upon her death. It took a long time, before I realised that she would be looking down on me and praising me for how I have bettered myself over the last few years. She would have been very proud of me and I really miss her and wished I could have one more conversation with her, but that is never going to happen and it is something I have learnt to accept albeit a painful long-lasting experience.

I remember around that time my cousin had a Cocker Spaniel called Koko. She was a lovely dog and when I was feeling low, I would take her with me on long walks. She had an uncanny sense of smell and would come up to me and sniff around me and then jump onto my lap. This happened when I was feeling miserable or sad. She knew when I was feeling depressed and would always try to cheer me up. She would not stop jumping on me until I took her for a walk, and we would walk for miles and miles. The walks were very therapeutic as they helped to reduce my stress levels, clear my mind and reduce any anxiety I had at the time. She knew that the walks helped me and was always a keen volunteer to *'help'* and I suspect she had the bonus of running around in the woods and across fields with her nose to the ground, rooting out anything she could find.

I continued to work on my CV building and eventually, after a couple of work experiences managed to source employment.

Within my skill set I needed to learn various programming tools and one of these was WordPress. I had no access to help from others and therefore, decided to teach myself. I spent hundreds of hours studying online videos and tutorials, which having BSL as my main language, wasn't easy as these videos were in spoken English. After many hours of research and study, I became proficient at using the software and eventually became *'addicted'* to using it. It is the main software that I use alongside others for my job as a web developer.

Luckily, I am a WordPress nerd as using it every day helps me to relax, surprisingly it clears my mind and any negativity is stored away until eventually it disappears.

With these skills, I can design and build websites for both my own business and the company I work for who are amazing, and I do not say that lightly. They are understanding, cool and never ever put pressure on me or treat me differently. I am part of a small team and we truly are a team. It is an experience that is alien to me as in the past I have been treated dreadfully.

I was very lucky in 2018 to visit Brazil for a month and during the visit I explored both the highs and lows of Rio de Janeiro. Many people see Rio as the home of football, expensive shopping centres and the famous Copacabana beach. What a lot of people do not realise or deliberately avoid is the infamous favelas. The favelas are synonymous with poor sanitation, education, poor nutrition, and high crime rates. There are around 1.5 million people living in the favelas on the edge of Rio. The main and oldest favela is called Providencia and was founded in 1897 within 10 years of the Abolition of Slavery. At that time there were 2 million African slaves received at the port of Rio.

I knew from my research prior to flying to Brazil that I had to visit and learn about life inside the favella. I arranged through an intermediary to have an armed escort whilst inside a favela called Rocinha and its surrounding areas. This was advised if only for my own protection and safety. I was shocked to see how poor and disadvantaged these people were and it kind of made me reflect my life to date and I felt that all in all my life must have been better than those who had to live and survive (quite literally) inside Providencia day in day out. Poverty was ever present and was impossible to disguise, or make it look 'okay'.

I also did the usual tourist places including Tabletop Mountain to see and witness the Christ the Redeemer statue. This visit made me feel very humble and I became overwhelmed with the emotion of it all. The view from the top was incredible and I posed for photos standing on the edge and sitting on the edge with my legs hanging in mid-air. I have shown these photos to the interpreters I use on a regular basis and many of them were amazed at how close to the edge I was. Visiting Brazil made me have a different view on life and I was determined, upon my return, to be more positive and proactive with life in general.

CHAPTER TWENTY-SEVEN

THE REBUILT MIND

"Sometimes we must break completely in order to rebuild fully.

Trust your ability to transform."

- Unknown

If I look back over the years I would say that I had some tough times and somehow I managed to get through them. I still have the scars from the bad experiences and they are stored away safely in a corner of my mind. My mental health back then was all consuming and literally controlled my life, my lifestyle and my decision making. Unfortunately this was detrimental for me and was something that I needed to 'repair'.

Currently I am feeling more positive, I am living a healthier lifestyle and my attitude towards negativity is to take it with both hands and throw it to the side and move forward without having it drag me down like unwanted baggage.

I am fortunate to have a good job and a great boss and team to work with. I am becoming more sociable and now will go out with a friend or two for a drink or a meal. I think positive everyday and if negative moments occur, I don't panic, I take a step back and review the situation and then decide on how to proceed next.

In the past, I would have allowed the negative moment to consume me and grow slowly, internally which would make me have dark moments, leading to a state of anxiety or depression.

I have set up my own business which provides educational courses to assist others with similar issues that I had years ago.

This is my way of putting something back instead of just taking all the while. The courses look at mental health, social media platforms and the pros and cons of being 'socially active'. The course teaches people to be aware of what is fake news and scam awareness etc.

I am a much happier person and any thoughts of ending my life are buried deep in the past. The thought of suicide seems a million miles away. I am fully aware, that it is easy to have those thoughts *'worm'* their way back into my mindset. At all times, I am on constant alert and very wary.

My thoughts and decision-making processes are not a one fix shop. Everyone is different, and this book is just showing how I dealt with issues. If some of these solutions work for you then you are most welcome to take them onboard.

The important thing from all of this is, believe in yourself. Make sure that when you are feeling in a dark place, you seek help from others. there is nothing shameful about asking for help.

Be confident in yourself and think positively, as much as you can.

I would like to end this part of my story by reflecting on everything that has passed by in the last 33 years. Times have been tough and sometimes life has been fun. Sadly, a lot of my life has been a negative that still lurks in the shadows. I know, that if I step into that dark area of my mind, the light that is constantly glowing will be extinguished as easily as a candle is snuffed out.

Life is inexplicably confusing. I suspect that is intentional insofar as, making every day a challenge. I guess if life was straightforward and simple then it would become mundane and unremarkable.

As I mentioned earlier, the best attitude for myself is to move onwards and upwards and face new challenges with courage and tenacity. The following 2 quotes remind me of what and who I am, and I would like to share these with you.

"I am strong because I know my weakness, I am beautiful because I am aware of my flaws, I am fearless because I learn to recognize illusion from real, I am wise because I learn from my mistakes, I am a lover because I have felt hate and I can laugh because I have known sadness" - Rebecca Ann Totten

"I am who I am. Not who you think I am. Not who you want me to be. I am me." - Brigitte Nicole

ABOUT THE AUTHOR

SHAUN FITZGERALD

Shaun Fitzgerald is the founder of Deaf Minds Education, an online Learning Management System. The company provides online courses accessible to both Deaf and hearing participants. The courses look at educating vulnerable children and adolescents, guiding them through issues surrounding Mental Health, Suicide awareness, and online abuse.

He is a Web developer by trade and has been involved in creating and building many websites for major companies within and outside the UK. Within his book he shares his personal experiences of being

Deaf within a system that is controlled by hearing people.

Shaun is a recognised TEDx speaker, mentor and motivational speaker. He currently lives in England and continues to support Deaf adults and children, whilst working on more personal development books, in his spare time.

ACKNOWLEDGMENTS

Writing a book is harder than I thought and more rewarding than I could have ever imagined. None of this would have been possible without my mother. She was the first person to pick up the pieces. She stood by me during every struggle and all my successes. That is the proof of an amazing mum.

I'm eternally grateful to my mother. She taught me discipline, tough love, manners, respect, and so much more that has helped me succeed in life. I truly have no idea where I'd be if she had not taught me the life skills I desperately needed at that age.

I would also like to thank my family from my mothers side including; my uncles, aunties, cousins, great uncles, great aunties and grandparents for their continued support and love, not only just for me but for myself and my mother during tough times throughout my childhood and upbringing.

To Rob James who met me as a young man and guided me through to a life of self-discipline. He was there whenever I needed to talk and was almost a father figure to me. At that time I was very impressionable and Rob kept my feet firmly placed on the ground.

To Andy a good friend for around 9 years who has always been there for a chat and catch up. He is always happy to tag along when a beer is required and enjoys providing that kind of support wholeheartedly.

I would like to thank someone who wishes to remain anonymous. He has been a great support throughout the years as and when he has been able to. He knows who he is, thank you!

To all the other people who have helped in some way over the years, I offer my thanks.

I would like to say thank you to those who gave me a hard time during my life and who made hurtful comments towards me when not invited to. You might have enjoyed putting me down or tried to hurt me both physically and mentally. Your actions made me a stronger, confident person. Your actions made me a more positive person and you enabled me to rebuild my mind.

DISCLAIMER

These are my memories, from my perspective, and I have tried to represent events as faithfully as possible.

I have changed some names to protect individuals' privacy.

To maintain the anonymity of the individuals involved, I have changed some details.

This book does not replace the advice of a medical professional. Consult your doctor before making any changes to your diet or regular health plan.

The information in this book was correct at the time of publication, but the author does not assume any liability for loss or damage caused by errors or emissions.

I have made every effort to contact all copywrite holders.

Printed in Great Britain
by Amazon